Blood, Sweat & Fears!

Rob,

Thank you for your SERVICE, and for the strength you show everyday. It is my honor to call you friend and BROTHER.

God Bless, NEVER QUIT, NEVER Forget.

Semper Fi!

USMC CEP

3/7 2010

No SHIT!

Blood, Sweat & Fears!

THE TRUE STORY OF 3/7, MARINE WARFIGHTERS, SANGIN, AFGHANISTAN 2010

———

Ronnie W. Alexander

ISBN-13: 9781539489887
ISBN-10: 1539489884

Table of Contents

BLOOD, SWEAT and FEARS!
THIS STORY IS BASED ON MY PERSONAL
ACCOUNT OF MY TIME SPENT AS A LEP DEPLOYED
WITH THE MARINES OF 3/7 DURING THE SUMMER
OF 2010, IN THE FRONT AND BACKYARD OF THE
TALIBAN IN SOUTHERN AFGHANISTAN.
I DEDICATE THIS BOOK TO ALL THE WAR
FIGHTERS THAT HAVE MADE THE ULTIMATE
SACRIFICE FOR OUR COUNTRY AND HAVE LAID
DOWN THEIR LIVES IN THE SERVICE OF THE
UNITED STATES. "THEIR DEDICATION, PATRIOTISM
AND COURAGE IS MOSTLY UNKNOWN TO ALL
THAT LIVE THE GIFT OF FREEDOM WHILE
UNAWARE OF THE BLOOD THAT HAS BEEN SHED
FOR THEM."
*(heard or read that, thought it was appropriate)

Author's Notes

———

The events that happened in this book are true, and recounted to the best of my ability. This is really not my story, but it is the story of the brave young men that I had the privilege to be with during that hellish summer of 2010.

I have tried to be accurate in the dialogue from my memory, but I'm sure that it is not word for word. The content is what I can recall, and is as true as I can describe it, based on time and place.

I have tried to be vague with certain information based on OPSEC and TTP's. Many of these men are still active duty and have moved on to other assignments that require certain anonymity. If you are not mentioned in this book, know that it was not out of lack of my respect for you or your accomplishments. It is just me, and my inability to remember, or get the real facts in time for this book to be completed.

To the Marines and Sailors that I served with, I am sincerely humbled by your Honor, Courage and Commitment. Thank you for helping me make it through and seeing this book come to fruition.

God Bless and Semper Fidelis!

Psalm 144:1-2

Blessed be the LORD, my rock, who trains my hands for war, and my fingers for battle; My loving kindness and my fortress, my stronghold and my deliverer; My shield and He in whom I take refuge; Who subdues my people under me.

Freedom is not free, but the U.S. Marine Corps will pay most of your share.
Ned Dolan

A Marine is a Marine. I set that policy two weeks ago - there's no such thing as a former Marine. You're a Marine, just in a different uniform and you're in a different phase of your life. But you'll always be a Marine because you went to Parris Island, San Diego or the hills of Quantico. There's no such thing as a former Marine.
General James F. Amos, 35th Commandant of the Marine Corps

I come in peace, I didn't bring artillery. But I am pleading with you with tears in my eyes: If you fuck with me, I'll kill you all.
Marine General James Mattis

"The British were chickens, but these new men... These American Marines... They fight like animals, like they're not even human."
- Intercepted radio transmission from Taliban commander, Afghanistan 2010

The following letters and awards were received by Ronnie Alexander from Marines and Sailors in his chain of command during his time spent deployed to Afghanistan with the Third Battalion Seventh Marines in the summer of 2010.

From Sgt. Maj. Steve Ahern USMC,
Former 1st SGT WPNS 3/7 during deployment:

Ronnie Alexander, former Marine, faithful and loyal, and a police officer. These are just a few of the accomplishments that Ronnie has achieved in his life, things he excels at. They're not too many civilians working for the Department of Defense, assigned to a forward operating victor unit who receives an award from the military for his actions in direct kinetic operations, but Ronnie has. Ronnie is my friend and I trust him with my life, but this trust wasn't given, it was earned by him. He proved that he could operate with Marines going into harm's way, and he did this on numerous occasions, whether it was engaging in direct firefights with enemy insurgents, or running into a field of fire to help save a group of blooded British Royal Marine commandos who were under direct enemy fire, or exploiting enemy IED and drug nests that were always booby-trapped. Ronnie always performed without hesitation and with cunning bravery. He personally saved lives and reluctantly took them when needed. The reason I know all these fine qualities and brave actions from Ronnie, is that he worked with me side-by-side, and with the Marines of the Third Battalion Seventh Marines during a highly kinetic deployment operation, in a place some people call hell, in the summer of 2010. You may have heard of that place, it's called Afghanistan. Ronnie is a great American. Semper Fi brother.

Signed,

Stephen Ahern Sgt. Major

United States Marine Corps

Certificate of Commendation reads as follows:

The commanding officer Third Battalion Seventh Marines takes pleasure in commending Mr. Ronald Alexander United States Marine Corps for outstanding achievement in the performance of his duties as a Law Enforcement Professional, 3rd Battalion 7th Marines, Regimental Combat Team 2, First Marine Division Forward, First Marine Expeditionary Force Forward, in support of Operation Enduring Freedom from 01 April to 01 September 2010. During this time period, Mr. Alexander executed his duties in an exemplary manner. Knowing that his skill sets were best employed on the scene, Mr. Alexander aggressively moved from between units spending over 120 days outside the Forward Operating Base during this period, with one stretch lasting over 32 days straight. These efforts directly contributed to the capture of over 500 improvised blasting caps, 1200 pounds of homemade explosives, 35 kilos of processed heroin, 256 pounds of wet opium, and numerous enemy weapons and munitions. During intense combat operations in southern Musa Qu'lah and Sangin, Mr. Alexander continued to be an asset by providing effective and accurate fire directly contributing to the elimination of numerous enemy fighters. Mr. Alexander's outstanding motivation and dedication to

duty reflected credit upon him, and were in keeping with the highest tradition of the Marine Corps in the United States Naval service.
Signed,
C. C. Tipton Lieutenant Colonel
United States Marine Corps Commanding.

Certificate of Appreciation:
As a Former Marine It Has Directly Enhanced Your Professionalism and Loyalty to the Marines and Sailors of the Third Battalion Seventh Regiment. Semper Fi. Once a Marine Always Marine. Thank You for Your Contribution in Support of Operation Enduring Freedom Helmand Province Afghanistan 1 April 2010 thru 26 October 2010.
Signed,
C. C. Tipton, Lieutenant Colonel
Commanding Officer 3rd BN 7Th Marines

From: LT Lance Stephens, (SEAL) MPAS, PA-C,
Naval Special Warfare Group TWO SEAL Team 10 Medical Officer
Subj: LETTER OF RECOMMENDATION ICO: Ronnie Alexander
It is with great pleasure that I write a letter of recommendation for Ronnie Alexander. Ronnie is an individual of dedication and integrity in both his personal and professional life. He never hesitates to go the extra mile to ensure a job is done right and to a standard far beyond what has been set.

I, Lt Lance Stephens, was assistant battalion surgeon for 3/7, one of the first Marine battalions in the 2010 summer surge to Sangin, Afghanistan. Ronnie was attached to the battalion as a hand-picked Law Enforcement Professional for his specific skills. Having worked with Ronnie in one of the most hostile and dangerous province's in Afghanistan I have seen him excel under direct enemy contact. It is without reservation that I say I would, and have trusted Ronnie with my life in direct combat operations. Ronnie became one of the go-to guys for the battalion for some of the most complex ops due to his unwavering professionalism and lead by example style. In representing the Marine Corps community Ronnie defines selfless sacrifice and the highest levels of skill and professionalism. Ronnie has served with honor and represented the Law Enforcement profession in an exemplementary fashion. He has devoted his adult life to caring for others and defending the freedoms of this great nation. Ronnie has my highest recommendation.

Very Respectfully,

L. Stephens

LT, (SEAL) MSC, USN

CHAPTER 1

Here I Go Again!

———

FIRST OF ALL, IF YOU'RE reading this book let me say thank you very much. Secondly if I've offended any of my current or former Marines by the descriptive nature of this book I apologize. Please let me try to explain how this all came to fruition. It all started 29 some odd years ago when I was blasted in the face by a Marine Drill Instructor. I had dropped and spilled the contents of my foot locker all over the front half of the quarter deck, directly in front of the hatch, of the Drill Instructors hooch. I was swarmed upon by two drill instructors and asked in the politest, and caring way," What is this cluster fuck, and what the fuck is your problem, you're a worthless piece of civilian shit!?!" Well, I really didn't know what a cluster fuck was, but I was smart enough to figure it out pretty fast. That term follows you through your everyday life in the Corps. If you were there with me, it all makes sense. If not, don't be a thin-skinned bitch, turn another page or two, and it will all become clear. The living, breathing animal that a Marine Corps Infantry Battalion becomes, as it progresses from pre-deployment training to combat, entails all the highs and lows, from the PFC to the BC. When I decided to call this book, "BLOOD, SWEAT and FEARS.....The true story of 3/7, Marine Warfighters in Sangin, Afghanistan 2010!" It was because, it was a way to bring to life, and the real stories of the brave Marines I served with. For the world to know about the everyday sacrifices made, and the story of the bravery shown by the Marines to my left and right on an everyday basis. Being a former Marine. I still love the Corps, and would never do anything to harm or tarnish that name and title I worked so hard to earn. I have been blessed to serve with some of the finest men, who are part of the finest fighting force in the world. I thank each and every one of you for taking care of the old fat guy through all we went through together. Hey bro, if you're reading this and were there with me in Afghanistan, and I don't mention you by name or by story, I'm sorry. Some days I just didn't get to write that shit down. I had to go by my own memory, and it seems like that's getting shorter every day. You all know if any of you ever make it down to Texas, I got all the barbecue and cold beer you can eat and drink. I owe you at least that much! Okay Marines let's get this thing going and prepare to push! I'm not a writer or author by any stretch of the imagination, so bear with me as you move through my story.

Lastly, I want to thank my family, who has stood by me or behind me (usually with a big stick) by helping me through everything. I could not and would not have been able to do this without them. I love you so very much and just want you to know that the thought of you is what got me through even the hardest days. Thanks for always supporting me in everything I've done. Also I know deep in my heart that it was the grace of God that guided and protected me through some of the toughest combat seen in Afghanistan in that hellish summer of 2010. Thank you to all the moms and dads for sending us your sons. Their sacrifice for me and the men I saw laying down their lives on the battlefield, will never be forgotten. Witnessing this, gave me a deep sense of conviction that it was not in vain or without purpose. I'm a Christian, but still a sinner and a Marine deep in my heart till to the last beat, so I ask everyone to forgive some of my language and inner thoughts I share with you as the story unfolds. Okay, enough of the lovey-dovey. Prepare to March! Break Break, Kill, Yut, Err, Semper Gumby, Moto, I love 'Merica', and all that other motivating shit! Well this is me, at the time 41 years of age, married, kids, house, truck, car, boat, motorcycle, etc. etc. etc.... But how did I arrive at this point. Stand fast and I will try and explain it. After my time in the Marine Corps, and my field experiment people call college. I became a cop in the Houston metro area. I was kind of a Gypsy cop, moving through different departments and doing various jobs for various reasons. I worked patrol, gangs and drugs, then as an investigator, and finally focusing on organized crime and narcotics. I had been blessed in my career, to do some cool shit. In the fall of 2006 I took advantage of the Global War on Terror, and threw my name into the money pot. As luck would have it, I got picked and found myself in Afghanistan doing PSD, mobile security and other cool guy stuff for the US Department of State via DynCorp. Had some fun, made a little money, paid off some bills, had some great vacation time, and got to do and see some really cool things. I also made some really good friends that year or so, as you always do when your life is in someone else's hands and theirs is in yours. Hey Jim, Spencer, Jeff, Corcy, Tater, Ray Ray, Huck, Bull, Dan and Gary. Can you believe I'm writing a book, yeah me neither? Okay I know I'm starting to wander, I will try and get back on track. So after I was done, I went back to Texas and back to work. Over the next year so I stayed in touch with some of the guys from my time in the Stan. All stop! Hey, if I sound vague with some of my dates and times and things I've done it should be obvious, Clearance or Op Sec, Huh? Are you tracking now? If you need to know I'll tell you, but you don't always need to know do you? Okay let's get back to it. Anyways, I was sitting back at the office in Texas, labeling the latest items from a search warrant we had just executed at a Meth monkey house from the night before. Well, all of a sudden I see the instant messenger flash on my computer, and it happens to be Tater, (Former Recon Marine and St. Louis Swat Cop) a buddy of mine from Afghanistan from my first deployment. I respond and asked where he is and how he is doing. Long story short, he tells me about his new job and says he needs a good man to help on the new job. It's a DOD job assisting the military in Iraq and Afghanistan with law enforcement training and investigations. Because they just don't have the skill set to handle the job in both places. We both agreed CID and NCIS have some good investigators and Intel can put the pieces together, but they just don't have the numbers to get down range where it's needed most. I asked where, when and how much, and the next thing you know I'm off to see the Wizard. The Wizard being the United States Marine Corps. Most military cops lacked the experience when dealing with organized crime and drug trafficking organizations, and that is exactly how the Taliban operates in Afghanistan. Using the funds made from controlling and selling approximately 90% of the world's supply of opium, the Taliban use it to finance their ongoing terror campaign. Having been in the dope world throughout my law-enforcement career that was right up my alley. Stand fast, tactical pause. I know I'm starting to ramble so let me get back on track. I wind up being hired as an SME, or subject matter expert, and sent to the Third Battalion Seventh Marines in lovely Twenty-nine Palms California. I will be a DOD advisor for the LEP program, or law enforcement professional program. We are to train and advise on all aspects of law enforcement, such as evidence collection, trends and patterns, corruption, drug smuggling, homemade explosives, counter drug and recognition, tactical questioning, detainee operations and many other things. From hands-on training and application at the squad level, but to the big picture scenario of what is what for the boss, or the Battalion Commander. So that is how I wound up back in Afghanistan again. And what a journey it would be, from moments of time filled with blood and sweat, fighting to live and save the lives of the Marines around me. Struggling to push away the fear deep inside me, to keep pushing forward, waiting to see the light at the end of the tunnel. If you have never fired a weapon at anyone in order to kill them out of fear or anger, then it's hard to relate to. The bond that you can build with these young men, be it Marines, soldiers, sailors, or airmen, is the bond of blood. When you have spilled blood together or you have cleaned up the blood of a fallen friend together, combat is that common bond. I don't know how many times in the middle of a firefight where there were IED explosions and incoming fire, RPG's with shrapnel and debris flying all around you, automatic grenade launchers peppering your ass or whatever vehicle you were in. I would look into the eyes of these brave young Marines and knew without a doubt that they would lay down their life for me or any other Marines that were with us. Not that they wanted to die, it was just a fact. They wouldn't just stand up and say ok I will die so you don't. No, what I mean is that they would grit their teeth and suck it up in one of the harshest combat environments in the world, and they would fight right there beside you to the bitter end if need be. I saw that determination and selfless sacrifice several times that summer. Right then and there that bond is made forever, never to be broken, not even in death. If you're reading this and you know what that bond is all about, then enough said. If not, then find a combat veteran and look them in the eye, stick out your hand and say thank you. That right there is the most that you can do, and all that a veteran really wants or needs, a little recognition and a thank you, it means a lot and goes a long way. I can never say and do enough for those Marines and Sailors that I fought with, and about those Marines that died in the summer of 2010 in Afghanistan. My door is always open, and I will always do my best to help them in any way I can. This book isn't about me or about what I've done or where I've been, I'm just trying to tell a story of what I've seen, and the heroic actions that I've witnessed countless times on the battlefield by the Marines that I was honored to be with. Shit happens in combat, things that you can't even imagine. After the smoke has settled, you stop and wonder - how the hell am I still alive? All I know is that we killed a lot of bad guys, and blew a lot of shit up in southern Afghanistan that year. The Taliban may not have known who we were when we got there, but they sure as hell knew who we were before we left. During the whole deployment, I never really got that feeling of dread or that feeling that my time is up, that my ticket had been punched. But, I definitely had those 'oh shit' moments when I was wondering what the hell I was doing there. Most of the time, things are happening so fast that all I could do is react, and thank God I had the training and memory to do what I was supposed to do. Not to just save my life and kill the bad guy, but to just suck it up and not let down that Marine on the left or the right of me. That was my biggest fear, to screw up that one big time, and the consequence be that I'd caused the death of a fellow Marine. Yeah, I know I was the old fat guy, usually bringing up the rear. But in my heart, I was still a Marine and I just would not or could not let the men down around me. That title - 'Marine', something earned a long time ago, is a title that I dare not tarnish. And being surrounded by these young hard chargers, all I had to prove to them was that I can pull my own weight and not be a burden to them, so they could continue to fight and kill the bad guys wherever we found them - which we did a lot. The Taliban were tough and fighting in their own backyard, but we took over and either killed them or pushed them out. The fun and gun would be fast paced. How fast I didn't know. You know that feeling going downhill on a roller coaster after the first big hill. It was like that, with more up and downs than you could count. Then throw in some blood and bullets, with the ever present IED. Goat fucker paradise was on the horizon. I just didn't realize the journey I would have to survive, in order to make it to the end.

CHAPTER 2

29 Stumps?

———

TWENTY-NINE PALMS, CALIFORNIA! OH, LET me count the ways! The Stumps, 29 Stumps, Desert Stumps, Shit Hole, the Sand, and oh yeah, and the.... Marine Corps Air Ground Combat Center. This is where my story really starts. It is the home of the Marine Corps desert training facility and some of the Infantry based units on the west coast, along with training schools for various MOS's related to supporting and training Marines. As all Grunts say, if you aren't Infantry you are a POG. Person other than grunt. Or, everyone else in the Marine Corps, is in support of the Infantry Marines in combat. This place is right in the middle of the Mojave Desert, and it is so close in the type of terrain that Marines will face in Afghanistan. The sand, the mountains, the grit, the heat, - and I mean hot! It really is the perfect place to train up Marines going to war in Afghanistan. Just surviving the training in preparation for deployment makes you tougher. Upon arrival I was ordered to the battalion office to check in and begin my indoc into the unit. I had to see the Operations officer (S-3) and the Intel officer (S-2), since I would be working jointly for both. But my ass belonged to the "Ops O", and he quickly made sure I knew my place and what was expected of me in quick order - no less explained in his caring and loving manner. He was a Mustang, a former enlisted Marine who became an Officer. I'm sure his first impression of me was less than stellar. I was an old, fat, former Marine. Captain Derrick Neilson was the Operations officer for the battalion, and he was a formidable guy with a no-bullshit demeanor and a straight forward approach. He looked like a Marine Infantry Officer should. Stout and strong, with a personality like sand paper. Period. I then proceeded to check in with the Sgt Major, Troy Black.

He was also a ramrod straight Marine with years of experience and a former drill instructor. No one needs to state the obvious about Marine Corps Drill Instructors. Just ask! They will usually knife hand you, then put you on your face doing push-ups or monkey fuckers. He welcomed me on board and then took me in to see the Boss, the Battalion Commander, Lt. Col Clay Tipton. Tipton is a former college linebacker and an infantry man to his soul. He is blunt, smart, and in control. There was no doubt in my mind from that moment on, who was in charge and how things would go in this unit. He asked about my background and laid down what he wanted and expected from me. He then explained to me in detail, how he would use my skills to find and kill the enemy. I shook his hand, then turned to leave his office. He crushed my hand and held it a second longer, looking me in the eyes. Being a former Marine, I still remembered how to take orders, and show respect to my superiors. I knew right then, that the lessons I had learned as a junior Marine, would serve me well, I was impressed and a little intimidated, but excited and ready to get started. He advised me to report to the 'OPs O' daily and to take his guidance on how to get me embedded with the Marines. The rest of the day was spent checking into the Battalion's different offices. First the armory, then supply, medical, so forth and so on. I remember going to the armory to check in and get a weapons card to draw my issued weapons. There I was, a nasty civilian standing in line with some Marines. When I finally made it up to the window to the Marine standing inside the armory, he just looked at me like I was crazy. I explained to him who I was, and I was authorized to draw weapons. He just didn't get it. I showed him my ID, then my authorization letter from Headquarters Marine Corps in Washington, DC. A few minutes passed, then the young LCPL took my ID and papers to a desk to make a call. He returned after I heard my name and several, "Yes Sirs." He still look puzzled, but grabbed a pistol and rifle to issue to me. I got squared away with the weapons and was issued a weapons card. I checked the weapons then handed them back to the LCPL, so he could place them back in their respective weapons lockers. As I was turning to leave, he told me he had never seen any shit like that before, then asked what I did. I grinned back at him, and saw a chance to fuck with him. I then said, "Son, that's a Secret, you don't have the clearance or the need to know!" I then turned and walked away, laughing to myself. I still wonder what the hell his was thinking! After making the rounds, I got in my government rental car and drove back to town to my hotel room, in lovely Twenty-nine Palms, California. I grabbed a beer and chugged it down. Sitting on the edge of the bed, I started thinking to myself, wondering how in the hell I was going to accomplish what I needed to get done. Could I even get the Marines onboard? What was my plan of attack? Finally I let it go, then got some much needed sleep. I would commute every day while training and working in the BN area. I would then push out to the field as needed for overnight or extended training exercises. The following day was time to meet the Marines and to get down to the Company level where my experience and knowledge could best be used by the men on the ground. I had to get my experience and knowledge down to the same level as the bad guys the Marines would be facing. I went down the line from top to bottom and realized that, this was make it or break it. It was a far cry from my time in the Corps. I had to take my sponge of knowledge and rub it on these Marines. The info had to get down to the lowest level to give them the edge that they would need. Marines join the Corps to get tats, get laid, blow shit up and kill bad guys. How the hell was I going to train these young Marines to stop and talk to people they wanted to kill, or look for evidence, when they could just blow it up? It was an 'oh-shit' moment. I had to earn their respect and confidence, then get them to drink the Kool aid. I wandered around the different Company offices, just meeting the men and introducing myself. I eventually met up with some of the KILO CO Marines in their office area earlier. I had told by one of the Lieutenant's that his platoon was in the barracks area preparing to conduct some walk through training. I walked into the barracks area for Kilo Company and met up with Sgt. Seth Rogers. Rogers was a lean, young, tough Marine that took pride in his men and his job. He was tough on his men, but I could see it was from caring, not from being a dick. He may have seemed like a hard-ass to the Marines, but it was the typical Marine NCO style leadership. We immediately hit it off, and he made it clear that whatever I had to offer his Marines would be another tool they could use to kill the enemy. So, I'm in the barracks lounge with 30 or some odd Marines, explaining to them, who I am, what I'm here for, and what my job is. I made it clear I was there for them, to train them to spot and identify evidence, how to collect it, and use it to link it to the 'big picture' bad guys so we could get capture or kill authority on the right dude. It was a struggle at first, but since I spoke 'Marine' fluently, I got my points across to them. After I finally got the big picture in their heads, it was pretty smooth sailing after that. I was lucky that I had some Marines with previous combat experience from Iraq and Afghanistan, that had done TSE or Tactical Site Exploitation, the same thing I had to get down to the lowest level throughout the battalion. Not only TSE, but Counter-IED, COIN, patrol tactics and so on. Where to begin but at the beginning! I had to access and design the knowledge I had and figure out how to push it down to the grunt. Down to the dirty, nasty, trigger puller Marine who only wants to kill the bad guy, get drunk and get laid when he gets home. Ok, I can relate, been there done that, but how to pound that into a Marine that doesn't know you or understand the big picture. You get down on the floor with your crayons and tablet and you start off with the basics and work up. You teach, then walk through every aspect that you can think of that might give that man the edge. If you send a group of Marines on a dismounted foot patrol, and upon their return, you will probably get a SITREP as follows:' No enemy contact, all Marines accounted for, and all sensitive items accounted for. No further information.' OK? I needed them to put their 'cop hat' on and tell me about the guy on the roof with the phone, the dude following the patrol in the adjacent alley, the shop with the 10 spools of double strand white wire, next to the shop with the yellow jugs, etc. Give me some damn Intel to chase, that can be turned into evidence, then used to kill that SOB that is using all that stuff to make IEDs to kill you. Not trying to change the "Kill the enemy mindset", but give them a different perspective that just might give them an edge before they get on the 'X', that one spot in time that goes 'Boom', that tears limbs from their bodies and drains the blood so quick that there is no time for good-bye. I've learned this in life. A shit sandwich with ketchup, is still a shit sandwich! Ok Ronnie, think you old MARINE! How the hell do I get these guys to believe what I'm saying? How do I get them to see it all on the move and still keep their combat bearing intact? Walk, crawl and then run. Believe me it was soon a trial by fire in the culminating event known as Mojave Viper, the litmus test for all Marine Infantry Battalions being deployed for combat in Afghanistan. Stand by because the shit is fixing to get real, and real fast.

CHAPTER 3

Mojave What?

———

So I'm sitting in the freaking desert surrounded by Marines for a thirty-day final exercise, before we deploy to the land of bombs and bad guys. I'm all over the damn place! I'm moving from company to company, trying to do my part to make sure the Marines are not only doing what I've taught them. But, also ensuring that they understand what they are doing and why. Don't think Marines won't bullshit you with a quick "Yes Sir", just to be done with your ass so they can get some much needed chow and rest. You don't have to like it. You just have to do it. That was the mantra I had to keep pushing. Believe me, I got a lot of 'fuck this' stares, some behind the back, and some "I am not doing this shit" attitudes. Luckily, I finally started to see it all come together when my Marines, and I say my Marines because they are my Marines, starting to do all the right things from instinct. The training kicked in and it began to flow. All the details became clear, and the young LCPL knew that he had to separate the bad guys and search them. The PFC knew he had to take pictures of the scene and fingerprint the bad guys. The CPL started collecting the evidence without being told, and then they all would come to me with a SITREP and a written report of the actions taken and evidence seized. It was a beautiful thing to be-hold. I was like a proud Poppa that had seen his boys grow up and do all things asked of them. But I think I was more pleased with the fact that the Ops O and BC gave me the head nod of approval, or a "good job LEP" response. As long as they were happy - all was good. God forbid I get called onto the carpet of the Boss. His disappointment or disapproval was quick and to the point. So pointed I could feel the criticism like a knife. He was hard but fair. All through the training and workup, Marines bitched day and night, just like all Marines.

They may bitch, but they get it done. They usually bitch while getting it done. I was encouraged by my progress, and hoped I had given the men another tool for their toolbox. Not one that would sit in the bottom drawer and rust away, but a skill that could be used to keep them alive and on their feet. The days and nights ran together. I set up training scenarios throughout the different stages of training. The Marines progressed through the various mock assaults and detainee operations. At first I had stay on their ass about attention to detail. On top of all the patrol and kill tactics the Marines had to employ, sometimes it seemed that my portion was pushed to the back burner. But eventually they started getting it right. I then started taking the lead on the different training blocks. We would patrol out through the MOUT town and look for and engage the "bad guys" wandering around doing obvious 'hinky' shit. Things started to click, and the boys began to perform the TSE/TQ tasks without having to be told or prodded with a stick. We started finding simulated IED's and weapons caches. Then we progressed to 'pocket litter' and fake ID's. All the little things that cops look for when catching turds. It was working. At about the five days and a wake up mark, we had just the final Battalion sized push to complete. We had to integrate every element of the Battalion into the battle plan, and to execute perfectly. Snipers, weapons section, air, comms, and the lowly grunt from the Infantry companies. All of them had to do their part to become a single fighting unit. I had been through every company and had been accepted - for the most part. I was seen as one of the guys and not just some old fat civilian dude that was a burden or hindrance. The shit I was spreading, was starting to make sense. That was so important to me. Anyone that is a current or former Marine, knows that it is a small circle, and you are either in it or you are not. I knew once I was in, I had it made. I knew that if accepted, I would be a part of the team, not the guy on the bench. Well, I was falling into the LCPL pipeline, and starting to question the reason why we were being pushed so hard by the Boss, LTC Tipton. It was a steady 'in your face' push of constant motion. Push yourself to the limit, then quit your bitching and keep moving. I mean, I never had it as hard as the Marines around me. I always got down time in between training exercises, but shit, I was old and fat. It was hell on my civilian body. But all too soon, the reason of "why" became crystal clear once we set foot on the battlefield. There were no more questions as to why this - why that? The answers were flying in your face at a daily pace faster than the speed of sound. The first time was an 'Oh-Shit' moment. But, I'm getting ahead of myself. I had made the rounds and got all the right checks in the box. So, I was good to go - or so I thought. When I had arrived at the Stumps, I was out of shape and not physically prepared to hump around with twenty-something year old Marines. But, my pride would not let me quit, I couldn't. With the end in sight, I ate, slept, humped, and ran through the desert with my hair on fire with my fellow Marines. It felt good and I was proud. So on the last day after the smoked had cleared, I was in good spirits and felt ready to take on the world with the men around me. Mojave Viper was wrap, done! Or so I thought! I wound up with Kilo Company and in the shadow of 1st Sgt Krauss, a tall lean Marine who has a huge smile and a giant foot to keep you motivated - if you know what I mean. It was decided that we would hump back to main side from the range area of Mojave Viper. I was like "hell yeah!" I'm good to go 1st Sgt! Then Krauss gave me a grin that said, "Are you sure?" Shit, I couldn't back down now, it was on, it was a Marine thing. So I grabbed my shit, slung it on my back, and got in formation as we prepared to push. Well, about five minutes later I'm thinking: "what the fuck are you doing old man?" I was in pain; my back, my legs, my shoulders. Damn! What the hell have I done? I was up and down the formation step after step. I was drained, but all of a sudden a Marine beside me slapped me on the back and said, "OOH-RAH Mr. Ronnie!" That's all I needed, some pure motivation. Motivation is a term used by warfighters to keep getting that last ounce of "fuck it" out of you. It got mine! I struggled and hurt and moaned, but I couldn't quit, not now. I think that Marine was as surprised to see me humping, as I was being there. Now that it was known, Mr. Ronnie was in the pack! I couldn't just quit. These men were going to be beside me when there was no option to quit. When quitting meant dying or worse, like getting another Marine killed because you couldn't hack it. Well, we made it back to main side at the athletic fields for final formation before we were turned loose. It was a quick affair, and thank God. As soon as everyone pushed out and cleared the area, I collapsed and thought I was gonna die, but I didn't. I had just killed one of the inner demons that lurks in the back of your mind, telling you to quit. I hadn't experienced that in a long while. It gave me that edge I needed to feel that something that gives you pride in yourself, knowing you had accomplished something you knew you couldn't. But the best part about it was when the Marines gave me a thumbs up or high five, or a Rah. That acceptance seared a brand in my soul that would only be challenged by what lay ahead. Well, the good times were fixing to roll and all would be well in the world of death and destruction. 3/7 was primed and ready to kill. From far away with Shadow (snipers), the CAAT weapons section, to the grunts on the ground, all elements were in place to be dropped in the shit hole known as Afghanistan. We weren't going there to win hearts and minds; we were going there to kill. Shoot em, stab em, hit em with a TOW, smash em in the face! Basically, we were hard chargers looking for a place to stick our boots and give the enemy hell. I keep saying 'we' and 'us', because I truly felt I was a part of something bigger than myself. And, I was proud of my place among the men around me. Little did I know, it would come to be one of the hardest things I had ever done in my life. But, it was also one of the proudest times in my life. Seeing Marines day in and day out do things that people at home have no clue or understanding of. You can't explain it to a tree hugger. He just wants to keep hugging that tree. Well 3/7 was not only going to make the grass grow green, it was going to give that tree all the blood it needed to grow. After some much needed pre-deployment leave time, it was time to get down to business. Business was good, too damn good sometimes. A Marine and his rifle are the ultimate killing machine in a combat setting. Well, the setting would be southern Afghanistan, Helmand Province, Sangin and other lovely tourist spots for terrorists and shitheads that needed killing. Stand by to stand by! Good night Chesty Puller, wherever you are! Old Chesty would be proud of the accomplishments of the Marines of 3/7 in the near future. Marines know their history. It is engrained into them from day one of boot camp - a common bond of brotherhood that can't be broken or lost. Something shared by Marines from Tripoli, Belleau Wood, Iwo, and Khe Sanh and very soon…. Sangin. The legacy you carry as a Marine is like a safe full of treasure. And, God forbid if you lose that treasure. Every action taken by a former Marine in a distant war from the past, is yours to carry forward, and not shame the good name of the Corps. It is each individual Marine's duty to represent the Corps past, present and future. And from my experience the future is still bright for our beloved Marine Corps.

CHAPTER 4

Kablamistan!

———

WELL, ALL GOOD THINGS HAVE to come to an end. And, by good things - I mean pre-deployment leave. It came and went as fast as a crack rock on Friday night in the hood. All our goodbyes were done, and that nervous anxiety started to set in. In the Marine world you don't show weakness. But being older and having a little more time under my belt, I could see it in the faces of the Marines around me. The ass grabbing was still happening, but it was just because that's what Marines do. We convoyed on buses south from 29 Palms to an airfield about two hours away. The reality was setting in and once we arrived, it was back to the business at hand. I had made fast friends with the Weapons Company 1st Sgt. Steve Ahern. A former Army dog and real world police officer, we hit it off real fast. He took me under his wing throughout Mojave Viper and showed me the dos and don'ts in regards to 'what was what'. Steve is tall with a face like leather after years of constant outdoor Marine fun and deployments. He is experienced and a world of silent knowledge. He was stern and quick to put a Marine on blast as needed, but he had that 'come here son' attitude that is needed to guide the Marines and accomplish the task at hand. We met up after we checked in and were standing by to catch the flight out. We shared a common need, snuff and coffee or cigarettes, so we got a cup and smoked. Then, we proceeded to expound on the ever present mission at hand. Steve told me that he knew the Marines were pushed to the training edge, but the first TIC or IED blast would be a wakeup call for all involved. I agreed and thought about what he said for a moment. As I was just about to respond, he blurted out: "Fuck it, it's only Kablamistan!" That term, Kamblamistan, would be repeated over and over the next seven months. I would use it to get a laugh or grin when around the guys or after an explosion had been felt. How little did I know, how much that term would play into our everyday existence over in the land of: Blood, Sweat and Fears! We made it on the bird and wound up in Manas, Kyrgyzstan at an Air Force base waiting to be pushed out to Camp Leatherneck in Helmond Province, Afghanistan. "Man-Ass" was uneventful and our last taste of civilization for a while. Two days later I'm sitting in a tent on the outer edge of Leatherneck. I wound up next to the "JUMP" tent, and began a close friendship with several of the Marines in the JUMP. The JUMP is the close protection detail for the BC. They go where he goes and provide security for him and whoever is with him as he travels across the AO. Since I had prior experience in Afghanistan work-ing close protection security, I started training and helping the JUMP guys with convoy security and close protection techniques that I had learned. They really embraced the training and asked about every possible scenario that they would come across. The main theme was getting off the X, coordinating com-ms and vehicle movement, as well as route Intel and clearance. I became espe-cially close to one Devil Dog, CPL Kevin Cueto. Being the redneck that I am, I always have a knife or two on me or at the ready, and I'm always sharpening them. Not really because they need it, but out of a nervous or time spending habit. Cueto was intrigued and asked me to show him how I got my pig stick-ers so sharp. Kevin could never quite get the angle right for the sharpness de-sired. I would show him again and again, but finally he said "Forget it!" He had this damn combat hatchet he carried and always talked about how he could use it or its need for various tasks he imagined. We would sit and talk and listen to music with my wireless speaker I had picked up along the way. Kevin was a fine Marine and took pride in himself and the Corps. He was excited to be a part of the JUMP element and worked tirelessly to hone his skills to the best of his ability. During off-time at Leatherneck, before we pushed out to bad guy land, he use to borrow my speaker for movie night. Nothing like seeing 8-10 Marines huddled up on a couple of cots surrounding a lap top watching a movie. It is a sight to behold; the noise, the smells, and the weird sense of humor. Kevin's courage and commitment would be tested throughout the deployment, and the sacrifice he made was a life lesson that I carry with me to this day. But, that tragedy will be made clear further down the line in my story. So, the daily grind of getting prepared to push out to parts unknown was getting tedious and boring. After all the training, preparation, and travel, the Marines were aching to get down range and prove themselves. Maybe a little too anxious for action, but hell, they are Marines. I wound up at Delaram, a small outpost that was on the edge of the Taliban controlled area. A few weeks passed and I was beginning to wonder when the time would come. As usual, you may get what you want, but you may not like what you get. Sweat, sand, grit, blisters, thirst, bugs and stupid shit were in abundance. Every day was just another step ahead into the abyss. Looking back at pictures and videos from the beginning of the deployment, you see kids, gleam in their eyes, clean uniforms, weapons shiny and new toys all around. Believe me, by the end of the next seven months, these boys wer grown ass men that looked like they had been put through the wringer. Not once, but over and over again. Uniforms torn, tattered and faded, falling off bodies that had dropped 10, 20 or in my case 50 lbs. The thousand-yard stare was common, and the everyday stupid shit was tolerated like it was normal. Dead bodies and devastation was not only in our future, but it would be what laid in our wake. I was anxious and ready to get down range and see bad guys up close. Being a former Marine was a fortunate advantage that I had from the Battalion perspective. I could follow orders, do what was expected and just tough it the fuck out like everyone else. My wellbeing and happiness was the far from the Boss's mind. How he could use me was another thing. I had heard horror stories about how other LEPs were turned into Fobbits and wound up stuck in a hut packaging evidence and pushing it to KAF or BAF. That's it! I was beginning to wonder if that was my future. I would bug the shit out of the OP's O, and then get I don't have time for your ass look, with a stand by response. Stand by meant, "Go the fuck away, I will tell you when you are needed!" Things were fluid and changing by the day. Looking back, the Boss was trying to figure out the AO, assets and bad guys. It's a lot of responsibility, and you don't always see big picture when you are a part of the picture. Finally, the day came for me to get down range and get a taste of paradise. I wound up with INDIA CO. in the Golestan area near Buji Bas Pass, in the heart of Indian country. We were at a COP about the size of a football field. Hell, maybe even smaller! I got there by ground convoy, and placed into a twenty-man sized tent. Next to me was a leader of men that I would come to love and turn to for an example of a warrior. SSGT Verice Bennett. Yeah, that guy! Marine to the bone, leader, tactically savvy, and a really good dude. On the other side of me was a Marine 2ND Lt. that had the most glorious porn name I had ever heard. It sounded like it was straight from an old school porn studio. "SCHUYLER NEWSOM -DIRK DIGGLER", it flows just like a porn stage name. You can't help but like that guy. He was oozing with the nervous energy that young Marine leaders are supposed to have. A handsome fit guy from Florida, we all hit it off well, and bonded almost immediately. Bennett and Newsom were the leaders for their platoon. Josh Waddell was another LT with INDIA. Josh and his Marines were set up further north from us. Verice and Schuyler had me train and coach their Marines every chance I got, and it was a steady flow of possible scenarios that I had seen, that could be turned into teaching lessons for them and their guys. I enjoyed the mentoring sessions, but I was ready for the teaching to turn into real world experiences. It would come soon enough. Every day was starting to prove that the enemy was real and out there watching. A week or two passed and the IED's became more frequent. Harassing IDF and small arms pot shots were getting closer and closer. We would foot patrol to the local village and meet and greet with the locals. All was as expected, and we set up a checkpoint on the edge of a wadi outside of the village, were three roads intersected. It was called checkpoint south. It consisted of a qualat compound and HESCO barriers. Being away from the flag pole, I had a little more juice with the junior officers, and was able to talk myself into going to the checkpoint so I could provide hands on guidance on the checkpoint operation. No one had any real guidance from above, on how to utilize me, so I would just see something that was in my lane and I would act on it. I had to do something. I was going crazy just hanging around on the COP wandering in and out of the TOC. I figured we could start stopping vehicles and looking for contraband. Shit, that was right up my alley. I loaded my backpack with essential items and jumped on the next supply convoy for the checkpoint. This would be my first taste outside the wire, and an early lesson on how fast life can be lost and friendships taken away. All I could think of were ways that my experience could translate to the Marines around me and hope that I could help in whatever way possible. I found out really quick that filling sand bags and Hesco barriers was a big help. It sucked ass, but it had to be done. My first scare was on a night I pulled security and almost caught the first golden BB slung my way. Hang on, that story is a good one and it sets the tone for the rest of the deployment.

CHAPTER 5

Checkpoint South

———

I WOUND UP AT CHECKPOINT south early one morning after bouncing around in an MRAP that was part of a convoy with gear and supplies. The checkpoint was still being put together and we had Marine engineers on scene placing HESCO barriers with a front-end loader around the checkpoint to be used as its walls. It was a little chaotic with Marines digging in, setting up firing positions, sand bags be filled, reinforcing the perimeter with razor wire, and just trying to get to a point where we could defend ourselves when or if the moment came. I met up with Lt. Gion and SSGT Medina, who were the assigned leaders of the checkpoint. Gion basically told me to drop my shit and help with whatever I could. SSGT Bennett had been on the convoy dropping me off and he was quickly assessing the situation with SSGT Medina, and they were giving Marines various tasks to harden our position. I dropped my gear and starting helping fill sandbags for fighting positions. As I was filling bag 1000, or maybe bag 10, shit - it was shitty work and it sucked. I looked over and saw a Marine that I had become friends with. LCPL Bobby Burns was an older Marine, 30 years old, so he had some world experience under his belt. Built like a Marine should be, athletic and in shape, Bobby was a guy I could count on at the LCPL level to help me get things done. We had met while I was taking a group of Marines to Ft. Irwin, a US Army base on the other side of the desert from 29 Palms. They had a dedicated TSE course that would certify the Marines assigned to each company's TSE teams. I had Burns and that crazy fucker Vincent Yeban, along with 30 other hard chargers during the Ft. Irwin experience. Yeban got sick during training and I took his ass to sick call. He was coughing, hacking, and crying about his labia being swollen. (Typical machine gunner pussy) About a year or so later, I found a prescription bottle with his name on it when I was getting one of my gear bags packed for another Afghanistan trip. I put it in my shaving/med drawer at home. Every morning I look at it when I get ready to roll. It helps to keep me centered and think about all you 3/7 boys every day. Thanks Vincent, love you bro. No homo! I and Bobby hit it off from the start, and he would become a close friend. Well, as Marines do, we got half-assed drunk at Ft. Irwin after training one night and I learned a lot about him. He was a former University of Alabama baseball player, grew up Mormon, and worked in Africa doing some vague shit with diamonds that he wouldn't elaborate on. So, seeing Bobby was a good thing. Dealing with Yeban made me drink more! I knew I had some guys that understood what I was trying to do and could be a big help. I just lucked out to have Burns at checkpoint south. After a couple of days of steady non-stop work, I and the Marines were freaking smoked. The engineers had hauled ass for some unknown important reason and left several hesco barriers unfilled. So, we filled them by hand with e-tools. Yes! Fucking E-TOOLS! Fuck my life! My fat body and soft hands were blistered and done. We finally got to a stopping point, but we still had to pull guard duty through-out the night. Sometime between us setting up on day one till day three, a group of 10 or so ANP (Afghan National Police) showed up to have a joint checkpoint operation. They were led by a slender young LT, with several other young police officers. All of them fresh from training - I'm sure. Well, we ate and worked together and shared duties amongst ourselves. The Afghan LT didn't have a flashlight and we always ate the evening meal together consisting of rice, beans, fried potatoes, and Afghan bread. It got dark early, and we all had to share our lights to get around. I had brought a spare headlamp, so I gave it to the young Afghan LT. It was pretty high speed and had high, low, strobe, and red light settings. He immediately became attached to me at the hip, and showed me great respect. I saw he took pride in himself and was a pretty strict leader of his men. He made sure they pulled their weight and al-ways helped the Marines when needed. As the days stacked up, the Marines were few and the hours were plenty. Marines were tired, but still had duties to attend to. I tried and helped with what I could, but shit, I was old and tired too. The next night at about zero dark thirty, a young Marine (sorry bro I can't remember your name), woke me up and asked, "Mr. Ronnie, could you finish my shift, these fucking rocks are talking to me?" What could I say but - yes. I got up, grabbed my rifle and climbed up to the M240 machine gun, which sat up on a wall. Just as I downed some instant coffee and got a dip of Copenhagen, an Afghan Police Officer jumped up there with me to stand post. I thought, ok that's cool. So, I grabbed my NVG's and scanned the area. The Taliban hadn't hit us hard yet, but they were sneaky and trying to get close each night to lay in IED's wherever we were at. Not two seconds later, I saw a blinding flash out of the corner of my eye. It was the ANP lighting a cigarette. A damn cigarette! Now anyone with any tactical experience knows that lighting up or any ambient light at night is a 'no-go', - period! Me being the patient guy that I am, I reached over, then knocked the cigarette out of his mouth, and crushed it into the dirt with my boot where it landed. I was making friends fast with my cultural diversity training. The Afghan glared at me and squeezed the pistol grip on his AK. I was thinking, FUCK! Here goes an international incident because one of us is fixing to get smoked and it wasn't going to be me. I pointed to the Afghan side of the camp and made it clear that he needed to get out of my sight. He did, and I turned back to my post just in time to see a burst of fire with greenish tracers coming from the wadi to the front right of my position. The exact reason you don't light up. You can give yourself away to bad guys at night. I was like, OK - it's on Bitches! So, I cut loose with the 240 for about three bursts. The whole camp came alive with Marines and ANP jumping up grabbing weapons and gear. The Afghan LT asked what happened through our interpreter, and after several tense moments, the threat had passed. I say passed because the pussies didn't show themselves. I finished my shift and the Marines changed out. The next morning, I was washing my junk with a baby wipe and getting water hot for coffee. I looked toward the Afghan side of the camp and saw a group of Afghan ANP circled around their LT. In the middle was the officer that had lit up the cigarette from the night before. All of a sudden, the Afghans lined up and the LT kicked the officer in question right in the ass and pushed him toward the other lined-up Afghans. They gave him hell with kicks, slaps, and a tongue lashing. After the discipline was complete, the Afghan LT, our terp, and the Afghan officer came and stood in front of me. The LT spoke through the terp and explained how embarrassed he was. He then slapped the Afghan officer across the face and yelled something in Pashto at him. He went to a stiff position of attention, apologized in Pashto, then stuck out his hand. I shook it and hand patted him on the back. He seemed scared to death, but I then grabbed his shoulder and told him through our terp, it was OK. No one was hurt and it was a hard lesson to learn and remember. He turned and sprinted back to his side of the camp. The Afghan LT shook my hand and wouldn't let go. I assured him that it was 'good-to-go' and he finally seemed satisfied. The Afghan CPT over the ANP made his rounds every 2-3 days and seemed to be on top of things. The 'word' or 'scuttlebutt' was that he was a Mujahedeen warfighter from the Russian times, and he was always looking to take the fight to the insurgents. Up north about 30 klicks, the TB had taken over a police station and killed several ANP. Intel said they were headed our way. The Afghan CPT always drove a Ford Ranger p/u truck, that we aptly called the "Danger Ranger". He drove the shit out of it - full speed ahead. He showed up and ate with us the next evening after the attack up north. We shared bread and rice and talked as best we could through our terp. He was respected and seemed to really appreciate the Marine presence there. The Afghan CPT was a hard charger. So, he took a group of ANP to go look for bad guys that might be in the area. The following day we got the word that the Afghan CPT had hit a large IED with the Danger Ranger. It nearly blew him in half! I was sick inside, knowing that he was doing what he thought was right. It gave us a wakeup call and set the tone for things to come. Our Afghan counterparts still needed training and guidance. To be honest, some weren't worth a shit and didn't want to be there. Others were ready to fight the Taliban, but needed more weapons and training. Things had been like a dream, all slow motion to this point, but we were fixing to be wide-ass awake. Keep reading and I'll keep writing. It's only going to get faster from here. Oh, and I haven't even got to the good part.

CHAPTER 6

Over the Mountain....my ass!

———

LT JOSH WADDELL, USMC, INDIA CO, 1st PLT, was a man child - thick, built for power, and smart. A leader and a get it done type of guy. His daddy was a SEAL and had served our country by sneaky and peaking in various shitholes all over the world for the past twenty some odd years or so. That being said, you know being tough was in Josh's blood. Based on the attack up north, and a fly over by coalition forces, we had Intel that a large unknown substance was on a roof top north of us in an out of the way village. It appeared to be HME or PETN that was laid out to dry in the sun. Waddell was with his Marines at another small COP in the Golestan area. Word came down for me to join up with Josh, locate the unknown substance, and to exploit it. Get a sample for evidence, the reduce it. That's military speak for blowing shit up! I knew Waddell had limited men. So, I got permission to take Bobby and another hard charger named Ranson Martel with me. This would be a chance to use our TSE training and get some real evidence. We briefed and got our truck assignments for the movement to the target. I wound up with some Marine EOD boys and we hit the road. ANA and ANP joined the convoy and we went north through the hellish terrain. Dirt, sand, rocks, hills turning to mountains, and it just kept going. After several hours, we made it to our dismount location, proceeded to get off on foot, and started humping. I was still soft and had no endurance. I was in Josh's patrol and he split the others to join the Afghan patrol. The Afghan patrol was headed down and around toward the target village. They had to go about 3-4 klicks around the base of a mountain, which we had set up to use as a blocking screen to cover our position. I was like - "OK". I can do a couple of klicks. I looked around to find Josh and get in the patrol element. Well, just my luck. I have to look up, and I mean way up, to find Josh. His ass was about 200 yards' vertical and headed up the mountain to get in an over watch position, till the other patrol had cleared and got ready to enter the village. I was thinking, this is gonna suck! And it did, a lot! I got my fat ass headed toward Josh and his guys in the patrol, and the more I humped - the farther he got. The patrol would stop and let me gain some distance. Then, they would keep pushing, higher and higher up that damn mountain. It finally got to a point of exhaustion on my part. Then, I realized that I was putting men at risk because I couldn't get my fat ass up that mountain. After about the third or fourth time waiting on me, I got on the radio and told Josh: "Fuck this, I'm going down and around, I will meet you there!" He 'rogered up', "Affirmative" and gave me a thumbs up. I gave him a middle finger! I headed down and around with Burns and Martel. As we were clearing the bottom and starting around the base of the mountain, I looked up and saw Josh and his Marines setting up their positions on the top of that damn mountain. I keep saying 'mountain'. Hell! It's probably just a hill in Afghanistan. But, to an east Texas country boy, that fucking hill was a MOUNTAIN! We finally linked up as a unit and approached the village. Josh and the ANA/ANP honchos met up with the village elder and we had a quick KLE to discuss why we were there and try to gather any Intel on the local shitheads. After the KLE, we pushed to the target building and linked up with the Marines pulling security on the perimeter. Myself, Josh, Burns, Martel, several Marines, and ANA/ANP cleared the building and proceeded to the roof top. Our unknown substance turned out to be just that. Either grain or some shit I can't remember. But, it was nothing to act on or destroy. After our little journey, it was a letdown. We took a break for water and to plan our next move. The moment we sat down, it was a steady shit show for me. I was harassed and given a hard time by the guys on my lack of mountain climbing ability. I took it all in stride, and it only proved to me I was one of the guys. If they were pissed, I wouldn't have heard anything from them. I was just thankful that my inability to hack it hadn't caused anyone to get hurt. We then proceeded back to our trucks and headed south. Along the way, we did a dismounted patrol at another unknown village in the middle of hell. At least it was hot enough to be hell! Upon our approach, children scattered and the place went 'ghost town'. That's not a good sign, and we pushed ahead at the ready. We eventually made it to the village center and sat down with an older local. His beard was chest long and white. He smiled and had his wife bring us water. I'm sure that was all he could offer. We thanked him in our best Pashto and we all acted like it was the best water in the world. I put the yellow jug up to my mouth and feinted a swallow for good manners. I was trying to be polite, but didn't want to get the running shits from the jug. After a while, we got up and did a foot patrol through the village and adjoining farmland area next to the elder's qualat. About two minutes into the patrol, a Marine called out to me that he had found something. I headed his way and came up to a small burlap sack filled with rifle ammo and a Chi-Com grenade. Lying next to that under the bushes was an immaculate looking British Enfield rifle wrapped up in another burlap sack. It was probably 100 years old, but it was in great shape. The stock was polished, decorated with studs, and the action was clean. Like, recently cleaned. I never was able to link it to a bad guy, but it shows that it was there for a reason. I believe that it was the old man's rifle, and he had one of the children hide it while we were being given the water and smiles treatment. Probably had it all his life and was used for self-defense, but he knew as much about us as we did him. So it made sense that he would hide it. Hell! He probably thought we were the Russians coming to take his shit. All throughout Afghanistan, there are villages that have no contact with their government or outside people. If you were not blood kin, a tribal member, or from another local village, they didn't know you from nothing. The last time he saw foreigners was probably during the Russian invasion back in the 80's. We all loaded up and headed back to Golestan. From there, I went back to checkpoint south to carry on with the daily grind of checkpoint interdiction. I remember on one occasion we stopped and checked a mini-van at the check-point full of Afghans. We motioned for them to get out of the van and line up to be checked out. The van had a roll of hay on top of the roof, with two goats tied up next to it. There were three Afghan males sitting on the hay, and twenty-four more inside the van. Unfreaking believable! Twenty-seven dudes, two goats, and a huge bale of hay. Only in Afghanistan! A week or so passed, and word spread that a convoy was headed our way. I didn't know the why or the purpose of the convoy, but I was so low on the totem pole, I never heard the word till it was time to move. We saw the convoy approaching in the distance, the dust cloud, several hundred feet in the air trailing behind. Just more freaking dust to deal with. Like, we didn't have enough of our own. As the convoy entered the checkpoint, it stopped. I was looking out towards the trucks when I heard the voice of LTC Tipton yell out, "Where is the LEP?" I ran out to him and was told in his most caring way to grab my shit and load up - we are pushing out. Shit! Half my stuff was at the COP a few klicks away. So, I grabbed my weapon and backpack and loaded up as told. We entered the COP. I jumped down and ran to my tent. Nearly running over SSGT Bennett, I gathered the rest of my trash and headed back to the convoy. Bennett asked what was up, and I told him I didn't know. The boss called and I had to go. Roger that! Go! The convoy was full of Marines and ANA troops. All the vehicles were full and I wound up in the last truck with the Afghans. It was an open air transport with the cab up-armored and armored panels on the sides of the truck. Fuck my life! I ate dust for 8 hours in the back of that damn truck. By the time we made it to where the hell we were going, I was covered in the shit. My hair, mouth, eyes, and the crack of my ass. I can still taste that damn dirt. We finally came to a stopping point in the middle of nowhere in the desert. It was about 0200, dark and getting cool. I felt a chill and looked around to see 15-20 trucks scattered in a defensive coil. I saw the boss with several other officers near his truck making plans. The plans he made would get me some trigger time and bust my cherry at getting blown up.

CHAPTER 7

The First Boom!

———

I STILL DON'T KNOW EXACTLY where the hell we wound up. But my best guess is somewhere between Musa Quala and Deleram. I grabbed my shit, walked over, and talked to the Boss. It was going to be a clearing op. Push toward known enemy positions, close in, and destroy them by superior fire power. Reality has a way of grabbing you by the balls and shaking you awake. Well, my balls were grabbed and I was wide ass awake. LTC Tipton walked over and asked if I had everything I needed to gather evidence and turn it into Intel for reporting purposes. I gave him a, "Yes Sir!", and then proceeded to be led to an MRAP. The front passenger door popped open and I was greeted by a female Air Force EOD SSGT.(Her first name was Robin) At first, I was clearly surprised. I didn't know we had Air Force EOD attached to us. Apparently, the war on terror was taking its toll on Marine EOD, and our EOD attachment for this company had not made it downrange yet. I damn sure didn't know we had any females downrange. I regained my composure and introduced myself to the AF EOD crew. I was given space in the back of the truck and piled in. The female SSGT was the vehicle commander. There was a driver, the Vic commander, and the tech in the back with me. He controlled the EOD robot and comms gear. We hunkered down and got about three hours of shut-eye. I heard some rustling around, then rolled over awake. I popped open a door to relieve myself. I was trying to be quiet since we had a woman on board with us. I stood on the step rail and leaned out of the truck. About two seconds into my morning piss, the front passenger door popped open. I saw Robin stand in the same position as me, then lean over. She peeked over the door and said. "Good morning." I gave her a good morning and tried to squeeze off the stream. It was a little disconcerting to say the least. All of a sudden, I saw a stream of urine coming from under the door she was standing in. What the hell? Fuck it, I decided to finish up. We both stood in the doorways and peed. I got done, then heard her laugh. I finally got the courage to ask her how she did that. She grinned as she was grabbing a water bottle. She motioned for me to look. She used the water bottle to wash out a plastic cup like device with a tube hanging out of it. I'll be damned! I had never seen or heard of any shit like that before. Robin told me it was called a STP (Stand to pee) device for women to use in the field. Roger that SSGT! I'm old and had never experienced females in the field downrange. It was something that I had not seen in the Marine Corps. Wake up old man, it's the year 2010! Just before sunrise, we started to move toward a small cluster of qualats. I asked the Airmen if they had any idea of the battle plan. Basically, they were told we were conducting a clearance op, and we would trail in support to exploit any IED's or HME we came across. That was LTC Tipton's way of starting a fight with the local bad guys. He would present a target of opportunity to the Taliban, then when they bit - all hell would break loose by punching them in the face with a large sized fist of lead. This would be the first time with the Marines that I got a front row seat to a firefight, but it wouldn't be my last. I was talking and bullshitting with the Airmen, when I felt a huge pressure wave come over us. Then came the BOOM! The Marines had hit a roadside IED, not too big, but enough to get our attention and disable their MRAP. As soon as the truck went down, a DSHKM opened up to the front, along with an AGL. A group of fighters laid up in murder holes, then cut loose with machine gun fire on our left side on the left angle. A DSHKM or Dushka is a huge Russian machine gun that fires a round at you as big as a beer bottle. And an AGL is an automatic grenade launcher, an AGS-30 with 30mm grenades that are used by terrorists and other shitheads that want to kill the American way. I was like, "it's on now"! I looked out the small side window and saw a Marine CAAT truck move up and start punishing Taliban positions. In the distance you can actually see the pink mist of a direct hit from a MK-19 hitting flesh. It was a visual indicator that I was glad I was on the giving and not the receiving end of that stick. About 15 minutes into the game, the enemy fire became sporadic, and then slacked to nothing. We pushed forward, and Marines dismounted to clear the closest qualats. Marines with mine or high speed metal detectors pushed up to lead the way, doing route clearance for the guys on foot patrol. Radio traffic was chattering, and you could hear that air was on station. A pair of A-10's zoomed over us and showed that awesome cannon Marines love to hear when it's handing out huge pieces of lead - when CAS is needed. The A-10 is a game changer and an attention getter for insurgents dug into their holes. As the dismounted Marines closed in on the qualats, one of the lead Marines with the detector stopped and knelt down to inspect a possible hit. He called up a possible IED. The Air Force EOD truck pushed up to within 100 yards of the spot. All the Marines on foot pulled back and tried to find some sort of cover as they set up security. Being a grunt, I didn't have much experience with robots and high-tech gear. The young Airmen that was the robot tech immediately sprang into action. Getting the robot dismounted and set for a detailed search of the possible IED location. The female VIC commander spoke with the Marine that found the possible IED, and relayed the details to the tech. He got the laptop and a game controller connected and began to roll the robot up to the location in question. The whole time he was calling out distance and other info that was being recorded by the video. I was highly impressed with the Air Force EOD response and professionalism. It was obvious that they knew their job. They turned to and did it. Once the robot arrived, the tech performed a detailed search with the camera and robotic arm. Several tense moments passed and the tech advised he had a pressure plate and wiring harness. He then continued a meticulous search and located the yellow jug containing the HME. After bringing the robot back to the truck, he then grabbed a readymade charge of C-4 and det cord, and secured it to the robot. The robot returned to the IED location and placed the charge. The young Airman turned to me and asked if I wanted to blow the charge? Did I want to blow the charge? Not yes, but Hell Yes! He handed me the fuse ignitor and I grabbed the green cylinder with my left hand. He told me to grip it hard and to pull the round split ring on the end when he gave the command. He then pulled the robot back to a safe distance. After a firing call of, "Fire in the hole", three times he nodded and said, "Pull It!" I did, and the instant rumble from the blast rolled over us. It was cool as shit, and I was grinning ear to ear. Like, I had just defeated the entire Taliban all on my own. We pushed up to the blast area and did a quick BDA with the robot. After that, the tech physically inspected the hole and motioned me up. He helped me recover bits and pieces of the IED for evidence. We returned to the truck, as the Marines fell back into a patrol formation and continued to advance on the buildings ahead. As he broke down the robot to get it stored in the truck, I photographed, tagged, bagged, and processed the pieces of the bomb. I made a quick journal entry of notes for my report to be sent to Kandahar, along with the evidence, when we got to an area that would allow it. We loaded back up and maintained our trail position as the Marines cleared the buildings and set up a security perimeter. The morning turned into an oven, and the Marines loaded up into their trucks. We continued through the unrelenting desert and moved another 5-6 klicks towards another little village. The CAAT section branched out into an inverted V, with the grunts trucks in the middle upon approaching the village. My EOD MRAP wound up in position with the grunt trucks and in the rear. I heard a MA-Deuce open up from one of the weapons trucks, then the whomp-whomp of a MK-19 getting some. All of a sudden I could hear and feel a slapping sound hitting our truck. It was sporadic at first, Bam... Bam........Bam! The closer we got to the village, the more it picked up speed and precision. Bam! Bam! Bam! Bam! Bam! Bam! You get the picture! The Air Force crewed seemed perplexed at first and unsure what the noise was. I hollered up to the front of the truck and told the female SSGT, "We are being shot at"! She looked back at me and asked me if I could use a 240? I didn't say a word. I climbed up into the turret, charged the machine gun, and started looking for targets to engage. Looking back, I think she may have been asking the young tech beside me if he could get up and on target. But, being the person I am, it was an opportunity to get in the fight. I scanned the space in front of me and caught another MRAP pulling up on my right side with a 50 caliber in action. I looked over at the Marine and he looked at me, grinned real big, gave me a thumbs up, and re-engaged the bad guys to our front in the village. That was all the encouragement I needed. I followed his lead and starting putting bursts into targets as they appeared. I kept telling myself to revert back to my Marine training from long ago. I damn sure didn't want to smoke the barrel of the gun, or cause a malfunction. I kept repeating the old machine gunner mantra," Die Motherfucker Die!" I would squeeze, hold, release, and repeat. Upon every release, I would scan for bad guys and keep throwing love and happiness downrange. I know I hit several good targets and kept it up till no other opportunities presented themselves. I checked the feed tray and ammo can, then realized I was almost Winchester ammo. I called down into the truck for another ammo can. The young Airman pulled my pants leg and said he should take over. I reluctantly complied and crawled down. They AF was probably wondering who in the hell is this old fat dude up on a machine gun going all, "Full Metal Jacket!" Marines dismounted and got up close on the few remaining insurgents. The bad guys disappeared, and as quick as it started - it was over. The rest of the day was slow and involved after action reports and a hotwash with the Marine chain of command. We kept pushing through the desert looking for a chance to kill, but we didn't find any takers. We made it back to Delaram the next day, downloaded our gear, and cleaned up. The next few days were uneventful, just full of paperwork and evidence processing for me. I got my work done and stood by for the next evolution in the adventure that lay ahead for the Marines of 3/7. And the old fat guy always bringing up the rear!

CHAPTER 8

Lucky Lima and Desert Sand!

———

LUCKY LIMA COMPANY, ALWAYS GOT the short end of the stick. Shitty details and shitty locations! I wound up with LIMA in the lovely Afghan desert. It was kind of like being lost but with guns and explosives, and no one to kill. We set up our trucks in a security perimeter and stood by to stand by. Gunny Shawhan was a live wire type Marine, that used the knife hand with efficiency and then reinforced it with a sharp tongue. Hard to read, I had to take my time to figure him out. Once we connected, loyalty and help was always there when needed. CPT Nolan was the CO, and Jullian Kilcullen was the XO. Julie was a hoot and we got along from the moment we met. Lean and athletic, he was the opposite of me. My first day that I arrived back at the company area at 29 Palms, he showed obvious interest in what I was doing, and told me to let him know if I needed any assistance. Good Ole' Julie, I love that boy, he is a good man. I reached out to the platoon sergeants SSGT's Martinez, Gant and Valdez. Jessie Gant was a giant! Probably 6.5 240, bald headed, tatted former drill instructor. I would have had to whoop him with a stick, he's a big one! Francisco Martinez was a short, stout Hispanic that was a straight smart ass. He would make me laugh my ass off. He could talk shit with the best of them, and then he could back it up. Fearless and the counterpart to Gant. Mixed in the bunch was SSGT Joel "Tacticool" Riley. This guy had every known cool guy piece of gear you could think of. He had been a weapons instructor and was proficient with anything he put his hands on. Joel was the WPNS section SNCO for LIMA. We were both Louisiana boys (I was born there), and we had a common interest in weapons, beer, and pussy. Miss you Joel, hope all is well bro. I met Lt. Ed Kay, and Lt. Brian Coughlin. Both good young Marines tasked with hard jobs of leading even younger Marines with a smaller group of older experienced Marines. It had to be stressful. We started doing meet and greets out in the local villages. I rolled out with a mixed group of Marines and started heading toward a group of qualats. I saw an older Afghan male and made my way towards him. I was out pacing the security element and motioned for the terp to come up with me so I could greet the man. The young LT that was with us at the time, called out for me to wait. Mike Schroeder was his name. I think he was replaced by Chris Parks later in the deployment. (Not sure about that!) Mike came up to me and asked me to slow down. I guess he didn't want to be the guy that had the old fat civilian get blown up on his patrol. I told him ok, and waited for the Marines to catch up. My homeboy, Adrian Lamont Childress, "what up?" I think was in the group of Marines. Adrian was from Dayton, Texas in Liberty County. I lived on the north end of the county, he was from the south. Adrian has been an instrumental part in my writing of this book. Thank you brother, I really appreciate you, and couldn't have done this without you. Childress was either with us, or I had saw him before we pushed out on patrol. I'm getting CRS bad gentlemen. (Can't remember shit!) Just wait, you will get it too! We finally got the security element up and in place, and I and the young LT approached the elder Afghan. He smiled and seemed content with our presence. We had the terp come up and begin introductions. Now if you have ever used an interpreter, it is vital that he translates every word verbatim. And even more important, is knowing the cultural inference when speaking and relaying information. I didn't know this interpreter we had. He was young and seemed unsure of himself. Me being the quiet and shy guy that I am, I stepped up and grabbed the old man's hand and greeted him with the common Muslim greeting of, "As-salamu alaykum, Peace be upon you". We were in southern Afghanistan, the heart of Pashto country. So I used my redneck Pashto. The Afghan smiled, and we continued to hold hands in the Afghan tradition. I turned to the terp and starting speaking through him. Asking how the man was, his family and his health. The terp turned to the Afghan and started speaking English! WTF? I looked at the LT and then the terp, I told the terp to translate what I said to Pashto. He said ok, shook his head, turned back to the Afghan and spoke English again. I stopped him and grabbed him by the arm and pulled him to the side. I asked the terp where he was from. He was from Kabul, spoke Dari and learned his English from comic books and the internet. Fuck me! Who the hell was vetting these guys? I fired his ass on the spot and told him to go sit down.(Not that I had the authority to fire him, but I was done with him on this meeting) I grabbed some water bottles and gave them to the old man. I told him thank you and good bye in Pashto, and we continued to push. SSGT Martinez came up and I told him what had happened. He told me that he would spread the word about the terp and work to get us a new one. It was early June and the heat was fucking killer. We pushed out and basically walked around the desert waving to local Afghans, and presenting ourselves as targets to whatever TB where in the area. After several hours I looked over to Francisco and told him I was fixing to pass out. He gave me the "fat pussy" look and called a halt. We grabbed some shade and leaned up against a wall of a compound. I had stopped sweating and had gotten chills. I knew I was on the edge of a heat stroke. One more beer and taco please! Shit, I drank water and the Corpsman came up and poured water over my head and my neck. I thanked him and sat there a few more minutes. In the distance I could see a few MRAPS cutting through the desert, headed toward our CP area with LIMA. It was Gunny Shawhan doing his thing, rounding up gear and ammo or something. Apparently Martinez radioed Gunny and told him to stop by and pick me up. I was embarrassed, but I was thankful. I was smoked and my fat body still hadn't gotten into the shape it needed to be in to patrol all day. I thanked Martinez and he shot back that smart ass grin and told me, "Get the fuck outta here". I still don't know if he felt sorry for me or just didn't want to carry my fat ass back to the company area. Once back at the LIMA CP area, I got some water and chow and took my boots off. Now that we were back at the company area, we had some down time to recoup and plan our next move. Giant Jessie came over and we started bullshitting and talking about where we were from and all that kinda stuff. Low and behold, he was one of my oldest son's Drill Instructors from his time in the Marine Corps. The Corps is a small world, and you cross path with Marines from the past all the time. We laughed and joked about various things and then played cards to pass the time. Every morning 1st Sgt John Calhoun would call out for Marines to "stand to". Stand to meant getting your gear on and set up a security posture to guard against an attack. It was a common TTP of the TB to attack at dusk and dawn. I was still in my poncho liner blowing off the order to stand to. I was startled awake by a boot kicking me in the ass. I jumped up and was staring Calhoun in the face. He was as surprised as I was. He said, "Hey Ronnie, sorry about that, but you need to get up just in case". Fuck, ok! I grabbed my shit and sleep walked my way to a truck and pretended to be at the ready. My daily morning cycle of coffee, snuff, and taking a shit was on hold. But wait! I had to shit! When you got to go, you go to go. I grabbed my ammo box and squeezed in under the front fender of the MRAP I was closest to. I squatted down and took care of business. With my rifle across my lap, I reached into my right cargo pocket for my handy baby wipes. About the time I was getting a first good wipe, BAM! We started getting hit by mortars! 3-4 mortar rounds dropped within 50 yards of my truck. There I was, in mid wipe, pants around my ankles, with IDF trying to kill me while I was taking a shit. Just my luck! I quickly finished up as best I could, and saw Kilcullen waving and hollering at me. He was pointing to the truck and motioning for me to haul ass and get inside the truck. I jumped up, grabbed my rifle, then my pants with the other hand and ran to get in the truck. Myself, Julie, McIntire, and about 10 other Marines piled into the back of the truck like cord wood. Stacked and laying on top of each other, ass to face and balls to feet. As we lay there listening, I could smell something that smelled like shit. Whichever Marine that was down by my feet starting making a gaging sound. Apparently I had stepped in my own shit in my haste to get into the truck. Some Marines were laughing and other were cussing and gaging. I was making friends fast. Eventually the mortar attack subsided, and we kinda just fell out of the back of the truck. McIntire was laughing his ass off and Kilcullen was shaking his head. I was red in the face and didn't know whether to apologize or walk away. We regrouped and a patrol was sent out to look for the TB mortar team. I went back to my box and buried my waste and cleaned my boots. Any time after that, it was a running joke with LIMA guys about Ronnie shitting on himself. Ha, Ha fuckers! I wound up with SSGT McIntire, and got a place in his truck. We were pushing out about 10-15 klicks to start harassing bad guys with his ANA team of Afghans he was in charge of. Before would could roll out, in the distance, we saw a huge dust cloud approaching us. Damn, what now? The sandstorm was from one end of the horizon to the next, and went as far into the sky as you could see. One of our K-9 Marine dog handlers grabbed his dog and threw him up into the truck I was in. The Lab was panting and nervous. Being a country boy, I love dogs and tried to calm the dog down. He wouldn't get still and was running circles in my lap looking for his Marine daddy (K-9 handler). He wasn't being aggressive, just wanted his buddy because he damn sure didn't want me. The dog wound up with his ass and balls in my face and digging his paws into my crotch. Just another fun filled day with 3/7. After the sandstorm, the Marine grabbed his dog and we prepared to push. We got on the road with about five trucks filled with Marines and ANA. It was getting dark and visibility was shit. We continued on and happened to catch the back side of the sand storm in the dark. We inched along trying to see our way to a clear path. Finally, Jeff (McIntire) called a halt and said we would wait it out. Thank God! Gunny PJ Stoural, SSGT Jeff McIntire, and Major Fitts were the lead advisors for the ETT, or embedded training team. Those poor bastards were like desert gyp-sies just wandering around the desert with the ANA. They fucking had to coordinate, plan, implement, and move with ANA and the BN on the OP's in the AO. It wasn't easy, I applaud you. I always had a blast with them. I just want to give them a shout out, and tell them I didn't forget em. Good dudes, and thanks for always having a spot for the old fat guy. Oh yeah, PJ, thanks for the awesome party in your suite after the ball in Vegas. I know I passed out on your couch, but how the hell did you get my big ass back to my room? (Allan Egstad, thanks for reminding me and being on point as usual) After the storm passed, we dismounted to get some water and stretch our legs. Nothing like being in a MRAP with your knees over your head and your ass bouncing around. I climbed down to pee, and walked out past the truck. Holy Baby Jesus! We had stopped our lead truck about 10 feet from the edge of a cliff. It was a straight drop down into oblivion. The hillside we were on, fell into the canyon about 200 feet down. We all looked at each other and gave each other a look of disbelief. We were lucky. Jeff reoriented our convoy and got us back on track. I wound up somewhere with another Marine element doing some TQ on a couple of bad guys they had detained. I printed them and gathered what information I could. Somewhere in the mix, I also remember being in a truck with Jake "Mouse" McMillin. He was a funny dude and kept me rolling. Whatever he lacked in stature, he made up with pure Marine bullshit and grit. Mouse was fierce and another lead by example guy. I got a pic of him sitting in the driver's seat of his truck after the front end had been blown off. I yelled up to him to show me some love. Being the guy that he was, he turned toward me smiling and gave me the one finger salute. Just like I said, Lucky Lima and the desert sand. The thrills kept on rolling, and the good times were only just beginning.

CHAPTER 9

Hey.... Wait for me!

———

MY NEXT INVOLVEMENT CAME BY accident. I say accident. It's not like I stumbled and fell into it. No, I was where I was told to be and doing what I was supposed to be doing. The initial plan turned into a marathon gauntlet of hopscotch through the Afghan desert heat. When time is of the essence, running place to place chasing turds, desert hopscotch sucks ass! I had stayed with Lima Marines, and moved to another desert vacation spot. We set up a perimeter, waiting on the word. I was with LT Ed Kay from Lima Company, a thin, unassuming looking young man. If it wasn't for the uniform he was wearing, you would never know he was a Marine. Quiet and never overbearing, he spoke in a low voice, and was always quick to consider his options when it came to getting on an objective. He used his NCO's experience and leadership abilities to delegate his intent, and it worked. But I would quickly learn he was a warrior at heart, and would kill the enemy without hesitation. He became a go to leader, and was always pushing himself and his Marines to finish the fight. At the beginning of the deployment, I could see obvious leaders in the group of young Marine officers scattered in the different companies. I made a critical mistake by assuming things I saw during training. But in the heat of battle, when the shit is coming at you, men are bleeding out, and you are under heavy fire, the real mettle of a man comes to the forefront. With LT Kay, I can say from my own experience, he is a man and a leader that has my respect and appreciation. Intel was reporting that a local village was holding 10-15 Taliban. This area was known for the heavy amount of IED's that were being placed against coalition forces. This included the typical white wire, yellow jug, and HME variation. It became a common theme for the type of

IED we would faced daily. The day was spent cleaning weapons, getting some water and chow, then the quiet before the storm moved over us. Finally, the ops order came down to our platoon. We would push out on foot at about 0230 in the morning, when only Marines and the Boogeyman are out and prowling around. We would approach on foot and set up till daybreak outside a cluster of 5-6 large mud qualats. The bad guys were using these buildings for a staging point to go do bad things to us. The exact building was unknown. So, we had to hold a perimeter, split our remaining men into two groups, and clear the buildings two at the same time. Being a cop, I know that execution on two targets at the same time, while holding security on other buildings, can be a daunting task. 'Murphy' usually rides shotgun so he can take a shit on your plans. Planning and execution are key elements and you have to know what the other guys are doing in your team. Communication is vital to execution. We pushed out in the dark and made our way to the objective. I was stumbling around trying to use the piece of shit NOD's I had been issued. It was a constant battle to see my way clear of rocks and bushes. I looked like a blind idiot stumbling around. We made it to our LP/OP position and waited for the sun to break the mountains in the distance. After much discussion with LT Kay and SSGT Cody Valdez, I felt we had the best plan in place to get the job done. Not that I had any say in the plan. I was just like the other LCPL's, waiting to be told what to do. Marines were set up and formed a perimeter around all the buildings. I was stacked in the rear of one of the clearing elements. When the time came, the signal was given and we approached our assigned building. We eased up to the outer wall, then inched our way to the front gate of the building. We gave each other the look and the hand signal was given to breach. The lead Marine booted the front gate and pushed it off one hinge to open it. We pushed through and scanned our sectors of fire. As we cleared the qualat, our terp pushed up with the LT and began giving voice commands to the occupants. A couple of men, several women, and children were gathered up and brought out to the open area of the compound. Marines continued to search and clear the adjoining rooms and found nothing or no bad guys. What the hell? We left some Marines to hold security and we kept clearing the other qualats with the other team until all was called clear. Scratching our heads, we hunted for evidence of Taliban, but none was located. Finally, some of the men of the small village asked to meet with the LT. We escorted them to one spot, while the Marines maintained a security posture. LT Kay, myself, and a couple of Marines, and our terp, met with the men of the village and starting asking questions. It was apparent that they were scared and had reservations about talking in front of some of the men in the group. After a few minutes of going nowhere with questions and answers, an older bearded Afghan told the men to go home and back to their business. I looked at the LT and our terp. They and their homes had been searched, and nothing was found. The LT agreed and sent them on their way, but maintained his Marines pulling security around each of their homes. After they left, the older Afghan began to speak to our terp and explain the situation. The Taliban had been in the area, stealing their sheep and goats for food, taking their water, and what little supplies they had. They harassed them and beat some of the younger men who refused to join them. The older man was obviously the village elder, and he said that he had forbid any of his village men to join the Taliban. It was only a matter of time before the threats turned deadly. He was scared and unsure what to do. He confirmed the enemy had been using his village as a staging point and that they would observe our movements from there. And as a matter of fact, he knew that they used two other villages in the area to do the same thing. Really? No Shit? Yes, really! He pointed in a northern direction and told our terp the next village was 4-5 klicks away. The LT checked his map and got on the radio. Off we went, on foot, heading to the village in question. Eventually we could see the spot on the horizon. By that time, I didn't know if it was a mirage or what. I was freaking dying. My dogs were barking, loud! The Marines spread out and approached cautiously. As we closed on the village, Afghans began running, hiding, and ducking for cover. Our cordon was set and the same tactics were used as before. We speed up due to no more element of surprise. We then began to enter and clear the buildings one at a time. After several no joy buildings were cleared, I heard a Marine call for the LEP. That was my notice to shag ass and see what was up. I entered the building and saw the remnants of a trash pile with opened batteries and several empty artillery casings. The evidence was clear that an IED maker was in the AO. I started scanning, then went outside. I saw another burned trash pile, with more evidence of sneaky fucker activity. I knelt down to begin my evidence collection, when another Marine called out for the LEP. Shit! WHAT NOW? I got up and moved across an alley way to the next building. The Marine was standing in the door way, pointing to a pile of something I couldn't make out lying on the floor. I scanned the area for any booby traps, then proceeded to enter the room. I approached the unknown pile and saw it was about 10 open boxes of writing pens, with the ink cartridges pulled out, and the outer sleeves cut into 2 inch sections. Next to that on the floor was a large steaming kettle full of tea, with 4 or 5 tea glasses. Some of the glasses still had hot tea in them. We had just missed the bad guys. Shit! What next? I immediately turned to the Marine posted by the door and told him the enemy was close - if not mixed-in with locals. I called up to LT Kay and advised him of what we had found. We started a meticulous search of the compound and located a covered-up spider hole near the back wall by the back of the compound. All throughout Afghanistan, former water source tunnels and holes have dried up over the centuries. These are then turned into caves and tunnels systems that the insurgents use to stash weapons and opium before they are smuggled in and out. Not only are they good for caches, they are great escape routes when they need to haul ass. It was pretty obvious that these guys had just hauled ass. Marines began searching the area and looking for other spider holes in the area. I came back and continued my search. By the open doorway, leading into the main part of the qualat where we discovered the pens and tea, I looked up to the roofline above the door. I scanned the area and saw something dangling down and moving in the breeze. I got closer and saw it was a piece of two-strand white wire. This was the same type being used as a component on most of the IED's we had encountered in the area. At first, I thought it could be live. But, I quickly saw that it was not connected to a HME source, ignitor, or battery. I got the closest Marine to help me find something I could use to get up on the roof. As I made my way up to the roof, I was thinking: "Shit, just what I need"! I kept thinking I was either going to get my fat ass stuck halfway up or blown off the roof. I was finally able to ease myself up and over the edge of the roof. What I saw was direct evidence of bad guy intentions and desire. There were approximately 50-60 homemade blasting caps laying up there. Where I come from in the police world, we would call that a clue. I quickly assessed the situation and came up with a possible scenario based on the evidence we had found. It goes something like this. The Taliban either saw us moving to the original village or bugged out to the next one - or they bypassed the first village and set up in the second one. I'm thinking the second version because they were comfortable enough to sit down for a tea and blasting cap making party. As we pushed into the second village, they set down the tea, threw the caps they had made on the roof, then hauled ass down the spider hole - or mixed into the village with the other locals. The blasting caps we recovered were crude but simplistic in design, and they worked. They used either gunpowder, or homemade PETN. Once they had the explosive of choice, they filled the pen sleeve, attached the wire, then BAM! You got a readymade blasting cap for almost the price of nothing. After processing and collecting evidence, I went back to the original spot where I had found the burned trash pile. I photographed what I saw and collected what I could. If I could get a good print or DNA, and get it into the data base, then maybe we could start connecting the dots on who the hell our bomb maker was in the area. Well, by this point it was getting dark and it had been a long day. But it wasn't over. We got chow and water, and then prepared to push again. We started back toward the CP where we had started over eighteen hours earlier. I was a zombie. My feet and legs were done. My body was on auto pilot. I don't know how long it took for us to get back, but I know we wound up patrolling for a bout twenty some odd hours start to finish. I was smoked. But mentally, I was proud of myself for toughing it out. I had a few, "wait for me" moments, but I didn't quit. We had disrupted some bad guys and got some good evidence.

CHAPTER 10

Here, there and yonder!

––––

OK, WHERE TO START THIS next episode? I guess from the beginning - where else? But before I get to deep in the weeds, I want to give a little recognition to a good dude. Doc Kyle Bisbee. I can't keep track of where he was throughout the deployment. But all I know is that, whenever I saw him during our adventure, he was always in motion. Whether it was running under fire to care for wounded Marines, or treating a sick Afghan child. Doc Bisbee deserves a pat on the back. Thanks again, and thanks for staying in touch with me. We moved around the area looking for more bad guys doing bad guy stuff. I was pleasantly surprised when I found out that I was going down range with CAAT white. SSGT Josh Ortiz was a lead SNCO who worked under 1st Sgt Ahern. I and Josh hit it off instantly. We had got along during training, but never had time to really connect. Now that we were working together, we had time to feel each other out. No! Not in that way! We saw that combining each other's approach was ideal for getting the job done. He had the guns, and I had the.......Shit I don't know what I had! Oh yeah! I almost forgot Patsy. LT Patrick Madden, all 5 foot something and as big as a popcorn fart. He was my lucky leprechaun. His guys and I made a bond that has been with me every day since. It was prime time for the processing and smuggling of opium and heroin. The harvest season had just occurred, and the Taliban and Al Qaeda were operating just like the Mexican cartels back home. They were stealing or taxing the locals for their poppy, or operating their own poppy fields. The money they made from the European dope market was their bread and butter for operating money. After every harvest season, the money was used for more fighters, weapons, Chechen snipers, foreign fighters, Chinese

AK's, Iranian bomb makers, you name it. I had preached the interdiction piece before deployment, without much traction. I guess the Boss was too busy looking to slay bodies, but we finally got in the enemies back pocket. We had moved around and finally settled in on a huge open area with villages spread out in a 10-15 klick area. We would push out in trucks, then dismount into split or satellite patrols. These types of patrols would keep em guessing. I started to notice that all the villages had connecting spider holes and that the enemy radio traffic would pick up the closer we got to certain areas of interest. The Taliban tried to speak in code, but it was basic shit. After several compounds had been searched, the radio traffic was steady. I told Josh we were onto something. It was either weapons or a dope cache. We loaded back up and approached another qualat in the distance. As we got within 500 meters, we took small arms fire and a few mortar rounds. Based on what I had seen and heard, I knew we were pissing off the right guys. The CAAT trucks opened up and we pushed forward. We finally dismounted and pushed into the small village and began clearing buildings. I and one of the young Marines searched a particular compound for evidence. Other Marines posted security while we searched. Bingo! We saw obvious signs of shitheads, and shithead activity. Brand new motorcycles, small arms ammo, spent artillery and illume shells, and hand drawn maps on the wall. As we continued to search, our terp ran up and told me that the radio traffic was steady and a Taliban Commander was yelling at his troops for not fighting to the death at the location we were at. That's a Clue! Apparently, the weapons truck shot the shit out of them and they hauled ass. They were still watching us and planning their next move or ambush. The light bulb went off and I knew we were missing the mother lode. I got a couple more Marines and gave them a quick sit-rep and told them we were going to search every inch of this place. Josh had his guys set up a good perimeter, and I got a TSE team together for the detailed search. We dug through every inch of that place. Finally, we located some radios and transmitters for comms and long range IED detonation. I even found a couple of American made tactical flashlights with the word 'POLICE' factory stenciled written on them. No telling how they got there. Still not what I wanted, so we searched again. Found more ammo and some empty tractor fuel tanks that were being used as containers for HME IED's. These fuel tank IED's could be fucking nasty. When they blew, the thin sheet metal casing would blast out huge razor like chunks in all directions. The wounds that they could cause would be terrible. We piled everything up, got an inventory, and pictures of the items. Our terp came back and said that the TB commander was still steady 'Bitching and Crying' on the radio. So, I stopped to re-group and think. What am I missing? My 'Spidey' senses were tingly! I told the Marines, we have to search again. That went over like a swift punch in the face. I got the, 'We already did it' look. But like I've said before, you don't have to like it, you just have to do it. We turned-to and searched again. We ended up in a little barn area, where the goats and animals were kept in the compound. It was covered in grain, hay, and animal shit everywhere. One of the Marines pulled out his Kabar (Marine fighting knife, used to pluck out the heart of your enemy) and began probing a large pile of hay in the back of the barn. About the third time he stuck his knife in the hay, we heard a solid thump. He had hit something solid. We looked at each other and smiled. Hey Taliban, lick nuts! I was shaking with nervous anxiety. I helped him move the hay back from the pile. Under the hay pile we found a false bottom made from planks of rough cut lumber. We pulled one of the pieces back cautiously in case of a booby trap or IED. Once I was comfortable that it was half-assed safe, I gave him a thumbs up to proceed. Sweat was dripping of my forehead. The Marine pulled the other planks aside and there it was. Jackpot Bitches! Laying there in all of its pretty, Opium Glory, was about two hundred pounds of wet opium waiting to be processed and sold. That was why the Taliban commander was losing his mind. We had just taken his operational funds for this area. He was going to have to answer to someone higher than him about losing this to the Infidels. Oh happy day! We pulled it all out and loaded it up in one of the trucks. The TB radio was going bat-shit crazy. Fuck em! We then destroyed the other items in-place that I had not collected as evidence. I remember the guys driving one of the MRAP's back and forth over the contraband items. The tractor gas tanks were crushed like aluminum beer cans. It was a good feeling. We had hurt them in a way that would directly affect how they operated. But it gets better - way better. We headed back to our CP area and I started processing evidence and making notes for my report. Before we had found the dope, Josh and his crew had pushed out to keep hunting. As I was doing my thing, a Marine came up to me with a radio and said White Poppa was on the horn needing to speak to me. I grabbed the mic and called out, "LEP Actual to White Poppa!" Josh responded that he had found a large spider hole with connecting tunnels. TB radio chatter was picking up and he knew he was onto something. I told him what we had recovered and I thought he might find the same thing. He agreed and said they would continue to search. After about twenty minutes, I heard that they had recovered some bags of "stuff" and were headed back to us. I was like - ok, stuff is good I guess. I finished what I was doing and waited. I was finishing up with our haul, when Josh and his crew pulled up all smiles and grinning. They looked like giggling teenagers at a $20.00 dollar whore house, with a $100.00 dollars in their pockets. I asked what he had and what the stuff was. The boys were excited, and ready to show me. Josh had some Marines grab 4-5 bags from their truck and throw it down at my feet. I reached down and pulled a smaller clear baggie out of the larger bag. Holy Shit, Batman! The 'French Connection' didn't have shit on this dope load! (For you youngsters, the French Connection was a huge Heroin ring back in the day!) They had just seized over $20 some odd million in processed heroin. Yes, million! According to my redneck arithmetic, this dope, combined with the wet opium from earlier, had to be over $23 million in dope. This was no chump change - people! This was straight to the top of the Taliban checkbook. Josh got on the radio and passed up the word. I continued to pull bag after bag of dope out of the larger bags. It was packaged just like cartel dope from Mexico. It was vacuum sealed in clear one-kilo bags, with diamond cut slots so the buyer could see the product. I looked, and saw the heroin. It was all whitish-tan and in hard chunks. The bags were each marked with a stamp on the top and inside. It had the year "2010" in the middle of the stamp. On either side was a palm tree and the word "Arianna" above that. In the dope world, that was a maker's mark. It told the buyer that it was made in Afghanistan in 2010, and in the area of the Palms. So if it was good dope, the buyer would know where and who to get his next batch from. Well, the word spread fast up the chain about our find. LTC Tipton and Sgt Major Black showed up the with the Jump element. The Boss called me over and asked for a quick de-brief of who, what, where, and how. I ran the 'lick' down to him and waited for a response. (Lick is cop slang for good hit or arrest) I told him what I thought the street value was. I could see the skepticism on his face. He asked if I could confirm that somehow. I was on the spot and had to think fast. I'm sure he wanted the right answer because he didn't want bad info going up to command. Looking back, I can see that now. I grabbed my SAT-phone and called the Sheriff's Office back home. I told dispatch to connect me with Sgt Brian Nichols with the Texas DPS Narcotics Service. He was my old partner from the Narcotics Task Force. I heard dispatch connect me and then Brian asked if I was ok. I told him I was good but I needed some figures quick. I told him what I had and the closest weight I could figure without a scale. He put pen to paper, or finger to calculator, and asked again how much? I don't think he could believe it either. I told Brian again and waited. The Boss and Sgt Maj were standing over me like vultures on road kill. I listened to Brian's response and smiled, while trying to keep my Marine bearing in front of the Boss. I thanked him and hung up. I turned back to LTC Tipton and SGTMAJ Black, and told them that the current street value was between $24-26 million - depending on quality and supply. The Boss kinds chewed on that for a minute. He nodded his head at me, then I got a 'good job' as he turned away. Hell that was good enough for me. I walked over to Josh, told him the news, and slapped him on the back. Great job! We photographed the dope and I emptied one bag for evidence and possible fingerprints. I collected a dope sample, then I watched as a five gallon can of diesel fuel and a Willy Pete burned the dope to nothing in minutes. It was a good day. We had effectively taken money from the Taliban that could be used to kill Marines, or God forbid, innocent people back home. I was proud of the Marines involved and truly felt that my training had a direct impact on their capabilities. At least I hoped I was helping! The whole reason I was there was justified on that operation. As I continue with my story, I just want all the Marines to know how much I truly appreciate them. They truly are my brothers, and I am thankful for their courage and continued bravery they showed every day. You are always taught from day one in the Corps that, "Once a Marine, Always a Marine." I had always been proud of being a Marine. But, the moments to come would prove how true that slogan really is. It was an honor to be among these men, and it gave my life a purpose. It was something I had not felt in a long time. I did and saw things I never imagined. And, I was pushed to my emotional and physical limits. My experience with these Marines and Sailors during the next few months would be seared into my brain for life. It is not just a memory, but a part of me. I live day to day with these Marines in my thought. Thank you again. Now, Kill!

CHAPTER 11

The Cone of Jackassery

———

UP TO THIS POINT, I had been dragged around all over Helmond Province, Afghanistan. I had seen some shit and done some shit. But, the shit had not really hit the fan yet. After my last adventure, I wound up back at Deleram. I had a few days to process evidence and get paperwork complete. I did a storyboard on PowerPoint for the boss. So, I didn't get blasted, or made to do PT, or whatever he or Sgt Major Black were plotting against me. Besides, I knew that every waking moment they were plotting LEP maneuvers against me. Just waiting for the right moment to ambush me with the Op's O. Back inside the wire, I got to recoup and let my feet rest. LTC Tipton pushed the mantra of hard feet and strong backs. My mantra was more beer and soft ass. After a few days, I saw that the tempo of things was beginning to shift into overdrive. CPT Neilson, the OP's O, was in a mad rush as always and had no time for hugs. Even though I tried more than once to get a hug out of him. I was just lucky to survive those encounters without a throat punch. I met back up with 1st Sgt Ahern. We continued to debate and plan the proper approach to solving the world's problems. During the course of our discussion, the insanity of the situation was broken down in detail. Because, of course, our opinions really mattered to the people in charge. We bullshitted about the Taliban approach, the local response, and the corruption we saw at all levels from the Afghan government. We finally agreed that we were operating in the, "Cone of Jackassery!" It was an appropriate explanation to what we saw and dealt with on a minute by minute basis. It Stuck! Every time from that moment on, when we were in a screwed up situation, we reverted back to the Cone of Jackassery explanation. Standing there in a shitty situation, it seemed to explain away the unexplainable. It was a way to give ourselves a moment of levity when the shit was stacking up. CPT Carin Calvin was the CO of Weapons Company, a great guy who cares and always thought outside the box. He let his men make decisions and act. And, act they did! They acted like a bunch of wild ass Marines hell bent on killing anybody not waving Old Glory and singing the Marine Corps Hymn. What can I say? It worked! Our first incursion into Musa Quala was on an early morning. I can't remember all the details. So, forgive me if I get some things out of order. I believe it was 'early' early on 16 June 2010 when we all got the wakeup call. We all had been shot at by this point. But we really had not been 'Bloodied' yet! We were going into the Taliban's backyard, and starting a fight. Basically the area we were pushing into, was a hive of Taliban activity. The owned the land and controlled the populace. No one had ever really went hunting for them in their own backyard. Knock, Knock Bitches! The CAAT convoy staged a couple of clicks from where we were going to set up a company CP/TOC. It was still dark and cool out, around 0400 hrs. I was cramping and had bad vaginitis. I was feeling claustrophobic after the long ride and had to get out of that damn truck and stretch. Well I pissed, stretched, drank water, got a dip, and grabbed my woobie (poncho liner). I decided to just lay on the ground for a quick nap until we pushed at daybreak in an hour or so. You know when you are asleep but waking up, and the weirdest shit you see and hear just seems to be normal? Anyhow, that is what I woke up to. I heard loud radio traffic, shots in the distance, and a Marine trying not to yell, while telling me to get in the truck. He was flapping his arms and giving me the hurry up sign. I was like, fuck that! I'm trying to sleep and it is nice to stretch out. I think I was in Patsy's truck, or Josh's. Shit! I can't remember. But I clearly remember the Marine telling me, "we had to turn to now, Bailey is KIA!" WTF? OK, I grab my gear, get in the truck, don my vest, and shake the cobwebs loose. I then asked what was up. Apparently, the sneaky fuckers saw us coming and took some pot shots at us. One round got lucky for them, unlucky for us, and hit LCPL Michael Bailey. I didn't know Mike well, just in passing, with the little training time we spent together back at Mojave Viper. He was a former Navy man, and I heard he had been a 'Chief Petty Officer Select' or in-line for some type of promotion, before leaving the Navy. He decided not to re-enlist in the Navy and crossed decked over to the Marine Corps to be a war fighter and do what his heart told him. Got to respect that. Started off back at the bottom, had to go to boot camp all over again. Damn! I never heard a negative word about Bailey. The dedication he showed to God and country is a lasting reminder of a commitment to duty. All my brothers that made the ultimate sacrifice for me, and every other American breathing the air of freedom, owe them a debt that can never be paid. Sorry, I was rambling and had to clear my eyes for a moment. Fucking Afghan dust always getting in your eyes! We loaded up and pushed to the spot on the hill that had been picked out by CPT Calvin. Once we got set up, weapons set up a TOW on the edge of the hilltop overlooking the wadi. We had hills behind us and the wadi stretched for miles in front of us. To the left was qualats and buildings, then lush farmland and hills spread out for 10 klicks. About 1000 meters out front was two perfectly shaped hills that looked like titties. So, the first one was TItty#1 and the second was Titty#2. Of Couse! Then on the far right, across the wadi was a hill side that looked like a football, and a second one that looked like a potato. You guessed it! We called them the football and the potato. Remember these! They are important and will become relevant in the near future. So, with everyone in place, we began to scout out the spots and started picking locations and targets. About twenty minutes later, the young LCPL on the TOW called out PID to CPT Calvin. Calvin got eyes on the alleged target and confirmed what the LCPL saw. It was a group of 3-4 Taliban at about 3900-4000 meters away. Right at the outer limit of the TOW's range for effective sighting. The Taliban thought they were out of range and could just watch us without impunity. One had a radio, the others had an RPG and some AK's. They were wrong! Dead wrong! After Bailey's death, we were just aching to get some and even the score. Though nothing can replace a Marines life, we were looking for pay back - plain and simple. The LCPL gave CPT Calvin 'the can I Sir, look', and Calvin responded, "Kill em, kill em all!" The LCPL engaged the TOW missile and it shot out of the tube with a cloud of smoke and a Whoosh sound. It seemed to fly forever. After several tense moments the Marine called out, "Wire break!" Which meant that the wire guiding the missile had broken, and it would continue to track on the last sight adjustment it was given through the wire before it broke. About two seconds later we saw a huge blast and a cloud of dust. No Taliban were seen on that spot after the dust settled. We all were high fiving and slapping backs. What a shot! It was a 'sit up and take notice' for the bad guys. We had a long arm, and were going to use whatever we had to reach out and touch them. We stayed for several more days and had some more engagements. It was steady move to kill firefights. The CAAT trucks pushed to wherever they could find the sneaky fuckers hiding and shooting. We got to see the bad guys in action, and they got to feel the boot of a Marine kicking their ass. I'm sure the Taliban were wondering who in the hell was kicking the shit out of them. We didn't just go away and hide when they shot at us. The WPNS boys would run toward them and blow the shit out of them. Suddenly we moved out, only to return to the same spot a little while later. We had a surprise upon our return, but so did the Taliban. They thought they could kill Marines and get away with it. They were WRONG! "3/7, No Shit!"

CHAPTER 12

Wooly Bully!

———

OK, SO WE MOVED OUT and went back to Deleram to regroup, and get more ammo. The word came down from on high that we were going back to Musa Quala. I was like - "ok, let's go". I grabbed my trash, then got on a truck ready to roll. The thought of Bailey was still fresh on our minds. We couldn't linger on it though. It only made the Marines more pissed off and ready to kill. We pushed out in a convoy and approached the same damn hill where we had made the bad ass TOW shot on the shitheads from earlier. We got set up and ready for what would be a kick in the balls. I wound up in a truck with Patsy and a Corpsman after several trucks had gone down to IED blasts. CPL Cliff Wooldridge and another group of WPNS CO Marines were spread out in other trucks, along with White Poppa and the crew. We were assigned to get down range and probe for the Taliban. LT Anis Abuzeid was another CAAT guy that was out rolling around in the mix looking to kill bad guys. He had his Marines on the prowl somewhere in the area. I got a good pic of him on CP hill standing there in his PPE butt naked. His pants had been ripped, and he was trying to sew them up when we started taking mortar fire. He jumped up with his junk swinging, trying to get those damn ripped pants back on. But that happened later down the line. We had figured out that if we took SAF from TB positions, they never expected Marines to dismount and out flank em. The only problem with getting on foot was the damn IED's. Once Marines dismounted, they would split or break off into satellite patrols. Patsy or Josh would coordinate by radio and the patrol elements would maneuver up and or around the bad guys. Then, they would smash em in the face - up close and personal. The Taliban were used to units getting shot at and blown up. Then, they would pull back. Or, the TB would hit em with a huge ambush set off by an IED, before trying to overpower them. That shit was just not going to happen to us. The sneaky fuckers had no idea who they were messing with. If I recall correctly, Jeff Mahaffey was with us as well. Cliff and Jeff had been roommates. They were funny to watch. They would get drunk and piss each other off. Then they would threaten to kill each other and beat each other's asses till they were bleeding and out of breath. Afterwards, they would go to bed and wake up asking "what the hell happened?" And they'd ask "how did I get this bloody nose or bruised eye?" But, God forbid if an outsider started shit! They did what all good Marines do. Protect and help your brother. We fight like brothers amongst ourselves, but we also face our enemies like brothers. Love you Jeff. Now, if you don't know the name CLIFFORD WOOLDRIDGE, that's ok. That's because his name is forever a part of Marine Corps history. His bravery and courage will be talked about throughout SOI East and West, and Marine Infantry Battalions till we are all a distant memory. Cliff is a full grown man from Washington state "lumberjack" country. Never boisterous or assuming, he is a Marine that defines what a MARINE is supposed to be. Diligent and determined, hard and strong, he is a Marine. Period! I am glad to say we are friends and I love him. Cliff is a quiet guy that seems to think before he speaks. When he does speak out, he means what he says and that's it. At first, I couldn't figure this kid out. He was always doing the right thing, but I hadn't broken the 'Wooly Bully Code' yet. I was always cooking and making coffee for the boys from whatever different groups of Marines I was with. I always coon fingered whatever unsecured food rations that were left open. Have you ever seen a Raccoon tear into shit and run off trying eat what they had stolen. Kinda like that. Just like in boot camp, you should not leave your foot locker unsecure, "now get on your face!" In war, the rules of 'have and have not' don't apply. I had secured these little canned hams from some of our British brothers, and some cheesy spread from the MRE rat-fuck box. Oh, and in case none of you knew this, Steve Ahern is the King of the Rat Fucked MRE's - Hands down! I never saw him eat a full MRE the whole time we were down range. He would grab all the shit Marines didn't want and turn it into some hideous looking mess. He would then eat it with hot sauce, or cheese, or peanut butter. Freaking wacko! I got into Patsy's

(Madden's) truck and got ready to get on with it. We headed down the wadi and toward the football and potato. We knew the TB had their spotters watching us and were just waiting to get off a shot. As we got closer to the potato, Cliff's truck hit and IED. BOOM! I can't remember if anyone was hurt, but they scrambled around and loaded back up in another truck. All set, we rolled out again. BAM! Another freaking IED! This shit was getting ridiculous! That MRAP was screwed and had to be recovered. The gunner from our truck pushed over to replace a wounded Marine and we lost another dismount to another truck. Finally, we got all the Marines reset in a new MRAP and were ready to push. I bet those fucking Taliban were laughing their 'Man Love Thursday' asses off, while watching us doing Chinese fire drills with trucks and Marines. Keep laughing bitches! It's coming! Now, if you know anything about Marine Corps Infantry operations, the following is not what you want. The following scenario could or could not have happened the way I'm going to tell it - at least based on the ramifications. This is how I remember it going down. Our Corpsman wound up behind the wheel, Patsy was in the front passenger spot as VIC commander on the radios, and yours truly was up in the turret on a 240. That's all we had! Three guys in our truck! After all the damn IED blasts and truffle shuffle of Marines truck to truck. I checked the belt ammo and feed tray. Then, I sprayed some extra lube in the upper and gritted my teeth. The snuff in my mouth tasted like a sponge with sand on it. Madden called out and the Marines rogered up ready to roll. Pushing again toward the potato, we starting taking SAF as we got closer. All of a sudden, a damn DUSHKA opened up and we were getting hit. Not sporadic fire either, but dead-on direct hits to the front windshield. I remember ducking down and seeing Doc scrunched down behind the steering wheel as rounds were impacting. Do you know how many rounds an up-armored MRAP can take to the front windshield from a 12.7mm DUSHKA heavy machine gun? SEVEN! I know this for a fact. The windshield was down to the last two laminated pieces after six rounds. Seven would have put us on the last piece of glass. The eighth would have penetrated and bounced around inside our truck. I was scared shitless and had to force myself to get up on the gun to start firing. I couldn't see exactly where the DUSKA was hiding. So, I sprayed and prayed a lot. The radio called out for all the heavy guns to lay down suppressing fire. Patsy coordinated and had the dismounted element get ready to roll. Cliff, carrying his SAW with a "Nut Sack" mag, got his Marines ready to go. All I knew was, I needed to shit and a shot of whiskey! Holy Hell! This was a no shit fire fight! I reloaded the 240 and kept a steady DMFD (die motherfucker die) cycle on the gun. In the back of my mind, I was proud of myself for not burning out a barrel or causing a malfunction. Weird! The stupid shit you think about while getting shot at. The TB were steadily shooting and locked in on our trucks. Cliff and the rest of the dismounts got down and started toward the target locations. They spread out and starting taking heavy fire. The Marines continued over open ground and ran into a group of 15 -20 Talibs. Cliff got busy with the SAW and dropped at least 8 of the fuckers. Pushing up to a qualat for cover, Cliff set up security to cover his Marines movements. As Wooly Bully held security alone, he heard voices and saw movement just around the wall where he was posted up. Marines were still taking fire and putting lead on targets. They couldn't get to where Cliff was posted up. Fuck it! A Marine has got to do - what a Marine has got to do. Cliff pushed around the wall and smoked the two closest Taliban, in the face and chest, from about 3-5 feet away. The third bad guy tried to run toward a back wall in the qualat. What is the old saying? Don't run, you will only die tired! He did! A fourth fucker had a PKM machine gun and took cover on the angle behind a wall. Cliff crouched back to re-load, when he saw the barrel of the enemy weapon come around the wall. What's a man supposed to do? Stand there and get shot? No! Cliffy-poo threw his SAW down, grabbed the bad guy's weapon by the barrel, then started face and throat punching the shit out of him with his other hand. They wound up on the ground, when the Talib reached for a grenade on Cliff's vest. Cliff gave him another lumberjack love tap to the dome and snatched the machine gun from him. Cliff got to his feet and used the weapon like a Louisville Slugger. He cracked the butt of the PKM on the head of the Taliban till he was dead. Not just dead! But, brains on the floor dead! While this hand-to-hand, up-close fight was taking place, the other Marines eliminated the few remaining Taliban. The Marines then moved to Cliff's location. Upon their arrival, they entered the compound and found Cliff standing over the dead Talib - with the other three sprawled out around him. Wooly-Bully had single-handedly killed 12-14 bad guys with his

SAW and bare hands. The few remaining bad guys had hauled ass and left the area. They were probably shitting their Man-Jams and high stepping it the fuck out of there. The Marines re-checked the area and humped it back to the trucks. We carefully drove back toward the CP, while keeping in our last tracks to keep from hitting more IED's. We figured that we had already done our own route clearance by hitting the other IED's from earlier. Once we got back and downloaded our gear, we had a huddle with Ahern and Calvin. Myself, Cliff, and Patsy grabbed some water and walked over to the command truck. I looked over at Cliff and saw bits and pieces of brain and skull on his hands and uniform. I didn't know what he had done at that point. He looked over at me and Patsy and said in a cool tone, "I think I killed that guy with my hands"! What? We got up to the CPT and gave him a hotwash of the engagement. Damn Son! What happened? After the brief, we grabbed more water and some chow. I made a batch of "Warrior's Stew". It was made of ramen noodles, cheesy spread, and the little canned hams cut up in it. I heated it up in my super-duper cooking cup. We stood together and passed it around as Cliff retold his story to the group. This story is now a legend in the Marine Corps. I am glad I lived through it and heard it told by the man himself. Cliff's actions that day would earn him the second highest award for valor - The Navy Cross! He didn't "WIN" it! He earned it! That's the legend and the myth - boys and girls. True story! I was there!

CHAPTER 13

Mohammed! Mohammed! Mohammed!

I HAD MADE MY WAY back to CP hill at the top of the wadi. It was hugs and kisses all around with Ahern, Calvin, and the rest of the guys. The action was steady and the Marines downrange were still fighting through ambushes and IED's every day. I got with one of the terps at the CP and started to take notes of bad guy radio traffic. The terp would listen and relay info to the CPT. Marines would then maneuver around to the bad guys. Otherwise, CAS or IDF would get on targets. The TB used dumbass codes and slang to talk back and forth. They would say: "they see our "camels" and "they are moving watermelons into position." Shit like that! We quickly learned that it translated into "our trucks" and "IED's". One Taliban commander had a group of dipshits that had moved back up on the potato. They were watching us, while directing mortar and DUSHKA fire down on Marine positions. I heard Josh giving out coordinates on the radio. Jets would come screaming overhead and drop 500 lb. bombs on the area, then pull away. After each bomb run, the TB commander would call out, "Mohammed, are you there, are you OK?" Mohammed would reply, "Inshallah! The infidels cannot kill us. Allah is with us", or some crazy talk like that. This went on for hours, as we punished them with bombs and mortars. Apparently they were dug in pretty good. After each bomb, we just knew we had hit them. But, I would keep hearing Mohammed and the TB commander talking back and forth on the radio after each strike. It was starting to grate on our nerves and piss us off. CPT Calvin had enough and eventually got a bomber on station. The bird rogered up and advised that he had 2-3 500 lb. bombs and a 2000 lb. JDAM! Oh Really? Oh joy and happiness! After the radio talk from the bird to the CPT and the FAC, (Eyeeore) we all sat there looking and waiting. Calvin grinned, Ahern gave a nod of approval, and I felt a little pee drip out. The CPT radioed back the situation to the pilot and asked for him to drop it all. Yes, all of it! The seconds ticked by, and we waited, and waited, and waited some more. Probably a minute or two later, we heard the bird overhead, but never saw it. A good hit was made on the target from a single bomb. The pilot asked if it had the right affects. No Mohammed was heard at first. We gave each other a thumbs up and thought we had sent Mohammed on his way to his 72 virgins. Not two damned seconds later, we hear Mohammed and his leader jibber jabbing on the radio again. Shit! What do we have to do to kill this guy? Calvin got that "Fuck it!" look on his face, and then got Eyeeore on the horn with the pilot again. The plane came back on target. This time he cut loose with the two remaining 500 pounders and the 2000 lb. JDAM! Now, if you have never seen the destruction that those types of munitions can cause, you could literally shit yourself upon impact. I know there is a good video that one of the boys got of the blast. It is a beautiful thing to watch. We watched in awe, as the destruction was thrown up hundreds of feet into the air. Forty-foot trees and thousand-pound chunks of rock and earth were blasted skyward. We anxiously sat and watched the show. Calvin told the pilot that he was spot-on and had good affects. The plane continued on and out of the AO. A couple of minutes passed - and no radio traffic. I grabbed the radio from the terp and brought it up to my ear. I looked down at the radio and noticed that I was gripping it so hard, that my knuckles were turning white. Nothing! Silence! I looked at Ahern. He shrugged and said, "That gives a whole new meaning to the phrase Kablamistan!" No shit, 1ˢᵗ Sgt! Just when we thought the radio was dead, the TB commander's voice yelled out - calling for Mohammed. "Mohammed! Mohammed! Mohammed! Are you there? Inshallah! Answer me!" Mohammed was too busy to answer - I guess. He was in paradise with his 72 virgins and counting goats, or whatever the hell dead Taliban do. Marines downrange pushed back into the potato area and did a BDA. The word I got was "total devastation". Body parts and pieces of weapons were everywhere. Good hit! Keep fucking with the bull and you'll get the horns! Late that afternoon, we took direct fire up on CP hill. We cut loose with the MK19 and 50-cal. After about thirty minutes of heads up fighting, the pussies slipped away to smoke Hash, drink tea and eat the chocolate starfish. After we had smoked checked

the potato, the Taliban were pissed off and seemed to want to get it on. Now, I don't know how true this next part is. But, I'm gonna tell it anyway. During the battle, additional Kilo Marines were inserted by chopper to help re-inforce and clear the area. They also had to support WPNS Co, due to them not having enough dismounts. I heard that it was the first time since Viet Nam that a Marine unit had been used to strengthen and support under fire by HELO insertion. I can't confirm if that was a LCPL rumor. But, I can tell you it happened. I was there and saw it myself. No problem! They had the right group of killers to give em what they wanted. Lt. Matt Perry, with Kilo, had been dropped in and pushed out into the Jungle. Matt and his boys were deep in the thick of it, surrounded by Marijuana fields and farm crops. With the steady onslaught of killing, we had pushed the TB to a breaking point. The Taliban had re-grouped and it seemed like they were hell bent on a Kamikaze type ambush of Matt and his Marines. Early on that afternoon, all hell broke loose down in the jungle. The Taliban cut loose with AGL and DUSHKA fire. Kilo was fighting for their lives. Matt kept calling CAS closer and closer to his position, as the TB advanced and gained ground. The radios at CP and BLADE Hill were steady with calls for support, but we had nothing but CAS and IDF to give em. At one point in the battle, it was reported that Kilo 3 was surrounded 240 degrees by enemy fighters. Shadow pushed up and started slaying bodies. The snipers probably killed 15-20 TB on their own. Fucking Shadow......
Kill! I heard Mafnas went all 'Bat-Shit Crazy' and started laying down suppressive fire till the barrel of his weapon was smoking. He exposed himself and shielded Marines by fire, while they pushed to an area to re-group. It was up-close and personal killing, with "Grenades, Bullets, and more". Jonathon Mafnas was another Marine that I had gotten close to during training. I brought him some PMAGS back from leave. He was freaking tactically proficient and smart. Mafnas and Art Osario would drill me for hours on enemy TTP's I had seen, locations, and the usual "this-that and then" - typical Marine shit. They are good boys and I'm glad to say they are my friends. The more of the bad guys they dropped, the more appeared. When all seemed hopeless, at least for me listening from the CP, HIMARS was cleared-hot. HIMARS is a big ass artillery round that's the size of a telephone pole. You can actually see it coming down on target. When it hits - hang the fuck on! It will rattle you to the bones.

I heard Matt call for the shot. CPT Calvin reconfirmed the request, knowing the strike would be danger-close. How close? We only found out after the smoke had cleared. The HIMARS came down with a thunderous bang, eliminating a butt load of TB. The effective strike opened the way for the Marines to eliminate the remaining threat, and to get on the move to re-inforce from a hard structure. The aftermath of the blast literally scrambled Matt's brain and some of his Marines. They didn't give a shit at the time. The fight was still on. They continued to fight. With the team effort of Shadow, Kilo, WPNS, and CAS, they were able to win the day. The snipers placed an American flag on a pole and stuck it in the ground where the main fight had occurred. It was an immediate visual motivator and a "Fuck You" to the Taliban. I believe another Kilo platoon was pushing through the football and potato area, when they walked into a shit storm. IDF from mortars and small arms fire engulfed them. They were in a running gun battle and made the way back to CP Hill and Blade Hill area. The spot where the Boss had set up was called Blade Hill.1st Sgt Krauss was pushing back to Blade Hill with some of his Marines. He took a bad wound to the arm from mortar shrapnel, along with a few other Marines. Big Daddy Krause allegedly commented on the fact that air burst mortars where dropping in around them. He got hit pretty hard and had a serious arm wound from shrapnel. Being the stud that he is, he got on the horn and called up his own 9LINE. I can still hear him yelling into the radio, with a firefight and mortars exploding in the background. You could hear Krause yelling back at Marines, "Kill those Motherfuckers!" CAS was close and laid the pipe to the Taliban. The next day, I was able to push out to Matt and his Marines for TSE. They had taken over several of the compounds the enemy had used during the previous firefight. Left over ammo and a few weapons were scattered about by the time I got there. We continued to search and located some cell phones, paperwork, and ID's. It was all good stuff for evidence and connecting the dots. At first, I thought, "Why the hell aren't the trained TSE Marines gathering evidence and getting it packaged?" Seeing the boys up close, I couldn't bitch at them. They were fucking smoked and I couldn't say a bad word to them. Let em rest and recoup. I got busy doing my thing. I was getting evidence photographed and collected. Shadow had pushed up and joined the other Marines. I high-fived them and grabbed Caesar by the arm. I gave him a hug and asked how he was doing. You could see the lack of sleep in his eyes, but he kept his Marine bearing intact. We smoked and joked, then we rallied up in one of the courtyards of the compound. After a while, I got up and walked around looking at the devastation of the firefight from the day before. The few compounds were surrounded by huge Marijuana fields - as far as you could see. I walked out into the Marijuana and pulled out my camera. Matt took a few pics for me. Then, Caesar walked out and stood by me. We got a few shots of us standing together in that field. I can still feel the heat and remember the smell. I grabbed my camera and took Matt's picture before we went back inside. Matt was starting to look dazed and confused, but he never let on that he was hurt. After my experience with IED's, I knew his head had to be killing him. He shook it off and continued to do what leaders do. Lead! I grabbed my gear and the evidence we had found. I made my way back to CP hill. Upon my return, I was tired. So, I dropped my gear and pulled my boots off. I reached into my bag. I grabbed my trusty Mickey Mouse sandals and my 'rubber bitch' that I had strapped to the back of my pack. I spread the sleeping pad out and pulled out my poncho liner for a blanket. I was so damn tired. Chow, coffee, or snuff didn't even sound good. Ahern asked if I was good to go. I nodded yes, and laid down. I don't know how long I was laying there. All of a sudden, I was being manhandled and attacked by some giant freak sex demon. That giant freak was CPT Alistair Howard. Howard was an attachment to the unit, and I still don't know what his big ass was doing there. CAG I think. We had hit it off from the start, and always had ass grabbing amongst us. Well, I guess my big ass looked good to him from behind. He had come up behind me and got into the big spoon position. Another Marine was at the ready with a camera, waiting for the right moment. The moment came when he plopped down behind me, grabbed me, and slung his leg over me. I thought the Gooks were in the wire and I was being drug off to be ass raped to oblivion. I tried to jump up, only to see and hear everyone laughing, as that damn camera caught me getting assaulted. Alistair! I still got something for you! After the sex games were over, I laid back down and got some rest. If I knew what was in store for me the following day, I probably would have stayed asleep. The next few days would turn out to be something I will never forget.

CHAPTER 14

What the hell am I doing here?

———

AFTER THE WOOLY BULLY ESCAPADE, I stayed on CP hill. A few days passed, and Marines were still checking for IED's in the area. Almost immediately, we found several pressure cooker bombs right in the same spot we were set up. The Boss, LTC Tipton, pushed out to us and 'the Jump' was clearing a path for his convoy to approach the hill. Kevin Cueto, being the Marine he was, was out front with a metal detector. He was working hard on clearing a path for his convoy. I was sitting beside the command vehicle when I heard a blast in the distance behind me. I looked back and could see a large cloud of dirt billowing into the sky overhead. Almost immediately, radio traffic picked up and a call for Corpsman came over the radio. The blast was only 200 or so yards away. I started to get up and try to go help in any way that I could. Ahern reached out, grabbed my shoulder, and told me "no". No? "What the hell 1st Sgt?" He pointed to the spots where the pot bombs were found and told me the area hadn't been totally cleared. I would not do anyone any good by getting myself blown up. I hated the answer, but he was right. Several moments passed, and the word spread that Kevin had been hit with an IED while doing route clearance. Shit! What was his status? No one had an answer, except that he was hit. I prayed in my mind and waited - and waited. Finally, the horrible truth made it to us. CPL Kevin Cueto had lost his life in the blast. Man! Why Lord? I was raised not to question God, but damn it, why? It was a hard pill to swallow. I sat there and cried. Kevin was my friend and a good Marine. It hurt, and being a father, I could only guess as to the anguish and pain his family would feel in the next few days hearing about Kevin's sacrifice. I tried to shake the pain away and refocus on the task at hand. We continued to set up gear and weapons systems for the fight that was coming. The Boss eventually made it to the hill and set up his trucks about 60 yards away. Kilo Company was in the area and Shadow snipers had pushed out to locate and eliminate bad guys. CPL Claudio Patino IV was a Marine's Marine. A trained sniper and leader amongst his peers. His skills and abilities were quickly known throughout the Battalion. I had got to know him and some of the other snipers during training and TSE classes. I taught them separate from the other Marines because they had to operate independently and on their own most of the time. They all took pride in their mission and were quick to learn. Patino always had a shit-eating grin and was ready to kill bad guys. He was a professional and always strove to be the best in whatever he did. I am thankful that I was blessed to have him in my life, if only for a brief moment in time. But that moment would have an everlasting effect on me. Thank you brother. After the blast that took Kevin, the shit started. Taliban started IDF and RPG attacks throughout the wadi area. Shadow had set up about 700-800 meters on a ridgeline past the titties, and were slaying bodies wherever they saw them. All hell broke loose on the ridgeline that they were on. I could see movement in the distance and hear a massive volume of fire coming from the area of Shadow. CASEVAC was called for from Shadow's location and a QRF rallied up from a compound led by SSGT Jorge Delgadillo. All fears were pushed aside as Marines scrambled to help out Shadow and get them the hell out of there. Patino was gone. Gone? It was unbelievable. I will get into more detail further in the book about the actions of Patino and Shadow. We had lost two outstanding Marines in one day. I sat there in shock and asked myself, "What the hell was I doing here?" I mean, I knew why I was there, but I was emotionally messed up. I tried to get a grip and push the anger and hurt away. I was able to get my mind right and look to the next task that would keep me focused. Josh, Cliff, and a few of his guys had pushed out to the titties and taken over one of the hill tops. They were under constant enemy fire and killed the enemy in bunches. I was sitting back at CP hill wondering how the hell I was gonna get into the fight. The answer would soon present itself. It was a steady diet of bullets and RPG's for the next few days. Marines would push out and engage insurgents and kill em dead. CAAT and Kilo were squeezing the TB into unfamiliar ground. That unfamiliar ground, was that the Marines would not quit or stop pursuing them. If they tried to hold a position, we would bomb the shit out of them. The remaining TB would flush out on the run and then be met by Marine rifle fire, or long range shots from Shadow. As the battle pushed back and forth down and through the wadi, Josh and a group of his Marines had made a home on one of the Titties. They fought their way there and humped a TOW system to the top of one of the hills. They dug in and continued to fight day and night. From the vantage point Josh had, he could coordinate CAS and get good strikes on the bad guys all through the wadi and adjoining area. I was going stir crazy sitting at the CP on the hill. Marines were pushed to their limits, but kept fighting. Our assistant Battalion Doc was a Navy Seal from Texas named Lance. He was a wealth of knowledge and a sniper. He interacted with Shadow and helped them with tactics and tradecraft. I and Lance became instant friends, and our love of hunting and fishing was just a few of the common bonds we shared. After a few days of just helping out by monitoring TB radio traffic, I was eating some chow and getting my head back in the game. I looked up and behind our CP area to the hills behind us. Marines were scattered across the AO. Only the command staff and a security detail was left at the CP. On the hillside, about 100 yards up, I saw a formation of rocks that looked like an arrow pointing up to the top. I looked closer and then about 30 yards past the arrow, I saw an obvious goat trail going straight up. MMMMM? Another clue! I got up and grabbed my rifle and walked closer to the hill. At the very edge, where the trail stopped, was what appeared to be a ridgeline with an embankment dug out. Shit! I grabbed my 'binos' and started looking closer at the ridge. Plain as day, I saw what looked like a reinforced entrenchment. Fuck! I went over to Lance's truck and told him what I found. He jumped down, grabbed my binos, and re-checked what I had told him. After he finished, he looked at me and said, "I think you are right." We didn't have any other Marines to pull to check it out. So, we decided to do it ourselves. We loaded up and started up the goat trail. Once we made it to the top, we found a huge entrenched ridgeline that totally circled our CP area. OMG! There were fighting positions every twenty-five meters or so. We found a command bunker dug into the hill with a stove and used supplies scattered around. We continued our search and located a supply spot that had a small hole dug into a hillside. I couldn't get my big ass through the hole. So, Lance crawled in and found some old mortars and 7.62 rounds. We huddled back up and kept looking. The whole hillside was connected by trench lines and different fighting positions. We couldn't believe it! Hell a couple of PKM's and RPG's fired from here would rain down hell on our CP. I took some pictures and Lance sketched out the layout. We took a last look around and made sure there were no bad guys hiding out. Pretty confident that it was abandoned, we 'exfilled' and got back down to the CP. We reported what we had found, and a Marine patrol was sent to recheck and clear the area. It was clear, but definitely put us on alert status. All I could think about was, what if the Taliban had staged an ambush from the higher ground on our first day back to the hill? Not only would we have lost Cueto, but no telling how many others could have been hurt or killed. Those sneaky bastards! After the loss of Bailey, Cueto, and Patino, the pressure pot bombs, RPG's, Mortars, and IDF we had endured the past few days, I was at a low point. All I could do was keep asking myself, "What the hell am I doing here?" Getting my bearing, I told myself to suck it up. What the hell else could I do? Call a timeout? There were no timeouts. There was only the realization that I was here to do a job. "Ok, Ronnie, get your head out of your ass and keep pushing." So, I did just that.

CHAPTER 15

Ortiz Hill

———

AFTER THE RIDGELINE INCIDENT, 1ST Sgt Ahern starting taking out his own patrols. He had a mixed bag of Marines, Corpsman, and ANA/ANP pulling security up at the CP location. He was not going to get caught with his pants down and took it upon himself to provide the extra security he felt they needed. Hell! I don't know how he kept it up. I never saw him sleep. It was CP, to patrol, to radio, to chow, and repeat - day in and day out. Finally, I had all the CP shit I could stand and told Steve I had to get downrange to help out some way. Ortiz had set up his crew on one of the Titties and was still there calling out targets. I got with Steve and Carin, the WPNS CO, and told them I could help out Josh. At least I would be in a central location for whoever needed TSE support. They looked at me with a shit eating grin, knowing I was just trying to plea my case to get downrange. Finally, Calvin consented and told me I could get on the next convoy going down the wadi. Hell yes! I got with Gunny Martinez to get the times to push out. Steve radioed Josh and advised him I was enroute to his location. White Poppa rogered up affirmative, and all was set. Nelson Martinez was the Gunny for WPNS Co. Talk about a tough son-of-a-bitch! I don't think he has ever, ever, EVER heard the word quit. He was in constant motion. He was always getting gear and ammo where it needed to go. A hell of a Marine, and I'm glad to say he is my brother and friend. Love you bro. Me, Nelson, and Steve rallied up by the truck I was in for the convoy. Steve told me to help with what I could but "No Hero Shit"! Gunny laughed, slapped me on the back, and told me to be safe. I loaded up in my truck and grabbed a seat. The back hatch and turret were still open as we pulled forward. The truck hadn't moved two feet, when a large blast came from under the rear driver's side tire. Shit! Shit! Shit! My ears were ringing and it felt like I was wrapped up in a bear hug from the "Rock". I couldn't see, hear, or breathe. The Marine that was up in the turret was blown clear, but I didn't know that at the time. We had just hit another fucking pressure cooker bomb. It was another welcome back gift the shithead TB had put up on the hill after we had left the first time. Apparently, it was a wet or bad charge. No real damage to the truck or Marine, other than the blast effects. We regrouped and went ahead with the convoy. All through the deployment, I had a habit of finding a spent ammo box and carrying it with me. At first, some of the younger Marines were wondering what the hell Mr. Ronnie was doing with that damn box. I always bungee corded it to whatever truck I was on. After the first time we stopped to take a break, I pulled the box down, dropped 'trow', and took a shit. It answered that question real-quick. I was too damn old to dig a hole and squat down. It would be just my luck to fall back into my own shit. No sir! Not me! Making sure my box was still intact, we pushed on down the wadi towards Josh. As we rolled down the hill into the wadi, we turned right toward the main open area and BOOM! It was another damn IED! WTF? Ok, we were all still alive, but the truck was toast. We listened for SAF or IDF, but none followed the blast. We dismounted and waited on a recovery truck. Another MRAP came and picked us up to finish the convoy. I grabbed my gear and shit box, then jumped on the other truck. Here we go again! We pushed on and got to within 200-300 meters from my drop off point. Josh's guys would meet me at the edge of the wadi and escort me back to their hill. Well, guess what? We hit another damned IED! This time, not only did it mess up the truck, but it blew up my damn shitter. I was pissed. Fucking Taliban, can't even let a man have his own private shitter out here in the middle of nowhere. Fuckers! The all clear was called and I dismounted. I saw Josh's guys on the wadi's edge and motioned for them to standby. A couple of the Marines with me grabbed some bottled water, batteries, ammo, and other supplies. I grabbed some water and batteries, then started humping it. We made it to the edge of the wadi and hooked up with the other Marines waiting for me. We dropped our gear and took a water break. It was decided that we would keep a low profile and help out with security till the recovery vehicle came for the last truck that was hit. Some of the guys were saying I was bad luck after being hit three times on one convoy. I poked back and some "kiss my ass and fuck off" remarks were shared. I still couldn't hear and the bear hug was now squeezing my head and chest. I was a little dizzy and disoriented. After the truck was recovered, we packed up and headed toward the Titties. The dry wadi turned into a lush tropical climate, the further we pushed toward the hill. Small irrigation canals ran everywhere. Marijuana and corn stalks were in abundance. We finally made it to the hill. I saw Josh and Cliff Wooldridge. We shook hands and settled down on the hilltop. Josh and the boys had been up on the hill for days and had been taking sporadic SAF and some RPG fire. From the hilltop you had an unobscured view of the entire battlespace. It was a perfect coordination point between the CP and to the other Marine elements downrange. With the TOW system and other optics, Josh was able to call out enemy movements and targets. CAS would scream in overhead and punish them with force. Or, Kilo and CAAT trucks would maneuver into a good ambush spot and lay waste to the TB. Shadow could coordinate long shots and surprise the enemy with perfect shot placement. One minute Habib was "screwing the princess goat", and the next he was bleeding out from a fist sized hole in his chest. It was a beautiful thing to watch. All the pieces were in play and the Taliban were getting their asses kicked. I got my gear laid out and found me a spot to occupy. The hilltop had a small trench line dug out and we had our fighting positions in place. There were several Afghan blankets scattered about. I grabbed a pretty red one for my sleeping pad. I had an old Viet Nam era spotting scope my daddy gave me. So, I pulled it out and set it up to help spot targets. Our radio operator was a dark green Marine from Washington, DC named Alonzo Brown. Back in the Stone Age, when I was in the Marine Corps, we were all called green. White Marines were light green and black Marines were called dark green. Sorry for the non-political correctness. But, it's my book and it is what it is. Cliff gave Alonzo hell day in and day out about the radio shitting the bed. Poor Alonzo was always changing batteries, changing freqs, or adjusting that damn wooden stick we called our antenna. The damn heat was hell on our battery life. Josh gave me the run down and told me what the current 'skinny' was. He would have a Marine scan the AO with the TOW. If a target location or bad guy was found, he would use his optics to range and get a direction. PID would be double verified, then he would pass it up to the CP to CPT Calvin. At the CP, we had a Marine pilot acting as a FAC. He would coordinate with CAS and hit the target. If CAS was not available, HIMARS or mortars would come into play. Otherwise, Shadow, or Kilo Marines, or a CAAT Wpns truck would engage the bad guys. If it was a really good target, we would win the lottery and usually get a combination of all the above. Sometimes, we could get indirect fire close to the bad guy and flush him out of hiding. Then, his ass was in a sling. They never could out run CAS, a TOW, or a .50. Shame on them! Their 'bad'! I got the picture and told Josh I had my old-school scope. I put it in play and started scanning the area. Now we had a third level of confirmation on shithead activity. Every evening, Josh would call up to the CP for our daily SIT-REP. He would start off with the details and pertinent info. Then, it would turn into a – "Good morning Viet Nam" - ramble of various daily comedy 'bitch' sessions. It was freaking hilarious and it helped to keep everyone level headed. It was like a daily stress relief sit-com. The word spread about Josh's comedy routine and pretty soon everyone that had a radio would stand by for the daily SIT-REP from the Titties. The hilltop we were on was Titty #1, I believe, or Titty #2. It was one or the other. Once Josh became a celebrity, it was affectionately known as - "ORTIZ HILL"!

CHAPTER 16

Heartbreak Ridge

———

A FEW DAYS PASSED, AND we were steadily giving the shitheads 'lead' in every form imaginable. We even had a group of local village elders come up to our hill. We didn't have a terp with us, but the message was clear. They kept holding their hands up with white cloths showing surrender. They would point out to a pile of rubble that used to be a qualat or compound. Eventually, one of them made it up to a Marine element with a terp. They wanted to bury their dead and just didn't want us killing them - thinking they were up to no good. Cool with us! Just don't go all Jihad and get any ideas! If so, we would give them another reason to bury someone else. I finally had some face time with Josh and the conversation bounced around about what had taken place over the past week. I told him about the IED with Kevin and how bad I felt. Josh is a good man and expressed his pain for Kevin. Then, I had to ask about the shit storm on the ridgeline where Shadow was ambushed and Patino was killed. Josh took a deep breath and shook his head. I told him how I could hear the firefight and see movement from as far away as the CP. After a second or two, he told me it took all his Marine Staff NCO discipline to not grab a group of Marines and try to help out. From Ortiz hill, you had a clear view of the ridge. He told me that he could clearly hear the gunfight and see Marines and bad guys. Radio traffic was going crazy. But, he couldn't get any type of IDF on station without it being friendly fire. It was hard to sit and watch. All he could do was pray and hope. We called it Heartbreak Ridge. I was told how Patino led a four-man Shadow element to a spot where he saw enemy movement, before he began to approach the top of the ridge. Almost at the same time, a large group of Taliban fighters were cresting from the other side. Both sides met at the top at almost the same time. From what I have been told by another sniper that was there, Caesar Ramirez, Claudio caught the first volume of fire and went down. Caesar immediately returned fire with his SAW killing several TB. It was a running gun battle between the two groups. The other Shadow Marines kept up returning fire and killing TB. Caesar continued to lay down a gauntlet of suppressing fire, as other team members tried to revive Claudio. At the same time, SSGT Jorge Delgadillo grabbed a corpsman and few Marines from the compound closest to Shadow - before he launched a hasty QRF. The Shadow team leader, SGT Coffey, moved up to assist and saw dead Taliban all around, where team mates were trying to revive Claudio. After two hours of dodging bullets, bombs, and steady IDF, the team was able to get Claudio's body to a CAS-EVAC location for recovery. Even through all of it, after running 1000 yards to get to him, Doc "PJ" never wavered or stopped trying to bring Claudio back. I'm sure having to 'let go' is a memory that will never be forgotten by the men that were there. Over the course of the gun battle, and attempted rescue, one steadfast Marine had lost his life. SSGT Delgadillo had taken an enemy round through the front of his hip and out his butt. That piece of hallowed ground, where Patino fell, will always be called Heartbreak Ridge - At least by me. The wave of heartbreak it caused would travel the globe to a family in Yorba Linda, California. Claudio's death touched us all. But I truly believe his fighting spirit spread over all of us, and more especially his boys with Shadow. They hurt, they cried, they asked – "why"? But, they pushed on and brought hell with them. Cody Wainscott, Jason Hall, Nate Coffey, Caesar, Bobby Cox, Brian Murphy, Doc Balacy, Pat Lorenzo and Billy Bob. All you boys have my everlasting appreciation for everything you have done for me. Not directly, but for the unseen sacrifices you made during that summer in Afghanistan. No one truly knows what you went through, or what you have done. I do, and I salute you. Days passed on Ortiz Hill and times were getting tough. Water, chow, ammo, batteries, and supplies were in short supply. Convoys were getting less and less frequent. We were almost combat ineffective when it came to vehicles. I don't know how many we lost to IED's, but it was a bunch. Now don't think we just laid down and gave up. Hell no! No trucks just meant we would hump it to wherever the hell we needed to be. So, Marines throughout the battlespace would push out on foot and continue to engage the enemy where they found them. The TB were starting to figure out that you couldn't go heads up with us. No way! So they reverted back to 'sneaky-fucker' tactics. There were more IED's, off-set RPG attacks, and mortars. They couldn't get close enough to hit us with direct fire or an RPG. Because if they did get that close, they usually wound up carrying several dead TB back to where they came from. Bleeding and with holes throughout, these bastards would get as close as they could, before launching an RPG up in the air at an almost 80-degree angle. They would try to get a trajectory that would splash the RPG rounds down on us. Sometimes it worked - sometimes they got shot in the face. After a week or so, it was a daily grind of searching for bad guys through our scopes and other optics. I had yet to get a TSE call-out because we were too busy killing. I had gotten into a grove with Josh and his crew. We had worked out a crude but effective targeting system. The effects of the bomb blast were starting to have consequences on my head. I had a constant headache that only got worse in the heat of the day with the bright sun beaming down on top of us. After the daily Ortiz radio show, we got the word that we had a resupply coming our way. That meant water, chow, ammo, and radio batteries. Thank God! At about 2300 hours, the patrol approached our position and made their way up to us. In the group of Marines was a Corpsman. Water and chow was handed out, then the other supplies. The Doc went down the line and checked on everyone. He came up to me and I told him to make sure all the Marines were good to go before he probed me. He laughed and said "no problem Ronnie, everyone is alright." Josh looked at me, knowing my head was splitting. Doc reached down and told me that he was going to check my eyes and ears from the IED blast a week ago. I poked fun and said he was shitty on time for house calls. After the evaluation, he told me I needed fluids and he was going to give me an IV. Are you sure? He nodded and broke out his gear. What the hell? Go ahead! He stuck me and I could instantly feel the cold fluid rushing into my system. It was instant relief and made an immediate impact. I remember laying there with Josh, Cliff, and Alonzo. Looking over Doc's shoulder at the bright Afghan moon shining down on us, I felt reinvigorated and energized. After the IV, Doc packed his trash and told us all to drink two bottles of water before we went to sleep that night. The patrol loaded back up and departed.

We all laid there and sat quiet, just looking at the stars and moon. I grabbed daddy's old scope and started looking at the moon in detail, all the craters and ridges. I passed the scope to Josh, then Cliff. We all small talked about it and made jokes. Finally, Alonzo wanted a look. So, I handed him the scope. He gazed at the moon for what seemed like hours. Cliff eventually asked Alonzo what the hell he was doing. Alonzo turned around and looked at us with the straightest face ever and replied, "I ain't ever seen the moon before, and that moon is big and bright!" Cliff responded, "Brown you are a dumbass!" We all just busted out laughing our asses off. Such was the life on "Ortiz Hill". The 'fun and gun' continued for the next week or so, and the adventures kept rolling. But, those are more stories for another chapter.

CHAPTER 17

Well water and chicken sketty

THE DAYS PASSED. KILO AND Wpns continued to hunt and kill bad guys as they found them. Shadow would deliver love packages by special delivery on unsuspecting TB that were still too dumb to stay hidden in whatever hole they crawled out of. Josh and the guys kept up with spotting targets and getting CAS on station. I started going out on probing patrols looking for spots that were still vulnerable to ambushes by the Taliban. On one of these little jaunts, I, Herbert, and a couple other Marines stumbled upon a small shop that had been abandoned. We relieved the shop of some soup noodles, cans of tomatoes, and the always lovely Pine cigarettes. This was of course done in order to deny the enemy any chance to resupply themselves. We finished up and headed back toward the hill. As we snaked our way through the canals and farmland, we took some potshots from three dipshits with AK's and an ICOM radio. Shame on them. We pushed up and took cover behind a berm next to a canal. Herbert dropped two of them with three quick shots. I was able to get the third one down, after seeing him trying to 'shag ass' because he watched his comrades transported to Paradise. We approached cautiously and searched them for pocket litter. I took fingerprints and photographs, while Herbert and the boys recovered the weapons and radio. After we finished, I noticed that one of the martyrs had a brand new pair of white Mickey Mouse shower shoes. I was like, "Surely he won't need these where he is going." I acquired the sandals and was happy that I had something to wear, while letting my feet dry out without hobbling around barefoot on the hill. We made it back to the hill in time for Josh's daily radio joke fest. I pulled my boots off and cleaned my new Mickey Mouse flip flops with a baby wipe and some hand sanitizer. I already had my own toe fungus working, and didn't think I needed to start a new strain of Super Afghan foot rot. I filled Josh in on our TIC, and started my evidence report and paperwork. I transferred the pics to another SD card, and bagged it in an envelope to attach to my report. We shot the shit and drew up the nightly over-watch schedule. I was on for the 0200 shift. FML! It felt good to let my feet air out without crunching rocks with my bare feet. We all broke out some MRE's and each ate what we could choke down. The cycle of the 'meals-ready-to-eat' was hell on my system. Depending on what you ate, you could go days without having to squat. And when you did, it was like a 10 lb. brick coming out a 1 oz. hole. Other times, it was like a lava flow on Mount St. Helens. You couldn't win for loosing. Then, mix that in with the local water source. We were always low on water. We kept the bottles we had used for various reasons. On one of our daily patrols, we had found a good water well in a courtyard area. It had a built on mud shack with a water shelf in a window. You would fill the shelf and it would pour out inside the little shack down a narrow funnel. It was pretty cool and well designed. You could have your own little shower. We took turns getting wet and cooling off. It was freaking awesome! The water well was deep and clean. At least it was clear. It was unlike the other water sources we had come across from other compounds. Herbert filled the little shower shelf for me, then I let him take a turn. We all lost ourselves for a brief moment in the coolness of the water. After we finished cooling off, we filled our empty water bottles and took them to the hill. Ok, so you caught me wandering and thinking back. Those moments with Herbert always gets to me. And all the guys 'in the know' - know exactly what I'm talking about. Love you brother. Rest easy. That tragedy is for another place and time. Getting back to eating our lovely MRE's on the hill, we assumed our scanning of the area with the TOW optics after chow. It had FLIR and could spot a heat source out to at least 4000 yards. We all settled in with one Marine on the FLIR and another pulling security. When my time came for watch, I got me some good old MRE instant coffee and some snuff. I had this bad-ass, mini-portable stove that collapsed into a one-quart cup/container. That sucker was a treasured piece of gear for me. It would heat water to boiling in about 45 seconds. I had bought about thirty of the small propane tanks before deployment. Then, I entered into a conspiracy with an unnamed 1st Sgt, who got them into country for me in their quad-con. You know who you are. Thanks Bro! Anyways, I got settled in behind the TOW and started my scanning. Nothing popped out at me. So, I drank some coffee and listened to somebody sawing logs. By this time on the hill, different Marines had rotated back and forth. Josh, myself, Cliff, and Brown were the constants. Herbert rotated down and I believe Giant Blakey came up the hill. I mean Elliot Blakey! Blakey looked just like Magnum PI with the 'manly man-porn' stash and all. Big boy machine gunner and a killer. I am glad to say that after we got home, I was able to give him a reference for a Police job back in Oklahoma. Proud of you brother. Keep up the fight! Anyways, my time on duty passed without any drama. After my shift, I crawled down to my little red sleeping pad and grabbed my poncho liner for warmth. The next morning, I started off with my daily routine. But not quite routine, I woke up to a damn goat standing over me. It had some green shit dripping out of its mouth while staring at me. Shit! I yelled at the goat and flapped my hands to shoo it away. I then found a spot to pee, brush my fangs and face, get me some coffee, and a dip of snuff. A country boy has to have coffee and snuff. Have to! The Marines stirred around, changed shifts, and what not. Our MRE box was down to the only meals that no one wanted to eat. The rest had been rat fucked and looked about as appetizing as a turd on a cracker. Somewhere along the way, I had secured a giant tea kettle and a big ole bean pot. Back home, it would be a bean pot. No telling what had been in that pot before I rescued it. I got to thinking and looking around. Down below our hill was 2-3 qualats that had been abandoned. I say - abandoned. The owner would come and go every few days to check his property, but I don't think he wanted to stay close to us. We were a shit magnet for the local bad guys. Well, down in the closest qualat, the owner had a nice little garden, some chickens, and goats. My redneck cooking skills were starting to kick in. I looked at the pot, then down at the chickens and the garden. We still had the noodles and canned tomatoes from the shop. MMMMM? What could we do? I grabbed up Blakey and another few Marines. Then, I told them we were going shopping for chow. They looked at me like I had a giant dick growing out of my forehead. I pointed to the pot, then down to the chickens. They grinned and got up ready to move. Have you ever seen a big ole 'Taliban killing Marine' try to chase a chicken in a war zone? It is a sight to behold. I almost pissed myself laughing so damn hard. After the chicken race was finally over, we had hunted and killed two chickens. Blakey was so damn hungry, I thought he was going to eat one of those chickens raw, - feathers and all. I said, "Hold up Killer, let me show you how Mamaw skins chickens." Mamaw being my grandmother Cupps from the deep east Texas piney woods. When I was young, the backyard and woods was our shopping grounds. So, I showed em how to pluck the feathers and skin those skinny ass chickens. Wasn't no Kentucky Fried Chickens here boy! We grabbed some onions and what looked like peppers from the garden, before making our way back to the hill. All the boys were excited and gathered around to watch. Josh asked what I was doing. I told him I was fixing to make some "CHICKEN SKETTY WITH WELL WATER!" He looked puzzled, but didn't have any quick come backs. So, I kept preparing the chickens. I started a fire for the pot and grabbed some of the bottled well water. I boiled the chickens, then cut up the onions and peppers. After the chicken was cooked, I de-boned them and put the meat back in the pot. The water had cooked up a good chicken broth. With the broth and chicken in the pot simmering, I put in the onions, peppers, and canned tomatoes. I had one of the guys grab a bunch of MRE single packs of salt and pepper. We poured that in the mix. Then, I added the noodle packs. I let it cook-down till it was thick and the noodles were done. I called out that chow was ready, and I almost got trampled to death by those wild assed Marines. Everyone grabbed a metal canteen cup or make shift bowl to get a portion. At first, everyone was quiet, just eating, and enjoying the moment. Finally, Blakey yelled out that this was the best damn chicken sketty in the world. And it was! It felt good to get some half-assed real chow in our bellies. Josh kept going back for more. So many times, I thought his big ass was gonna crawl in the pot. From then on, till the last days of our deployment, me and Josh - or whoever I was with - would always try and supplement our meals with some home style cooking. It was just another little way I could help out and keep the boys in somewhat good spirits. I remember some days that I didn't get to cook, and I could see disappointment in the Marines faces that had come back from patrol to only have a damn MRE. I always tried to have coffee ready in the mornings and at least a hot meal in the evenings. It made my heart feel good. It built another bond with the boys, and I am thankful for that. That my friends, is the legendary story of Well Water and Chicken Sketty! It was no big deal to do it, but it was a big deal to be a part of it. Ok, let's gather our thoughts, and get ready for another exciting tale of smoking, joking and killing terrorists.

CHAPTER 18

Patrol from hell!

———

IT ALL STARTED FROM THE moment I woke up to gunfire and shit blowing up. I had left Ortiz Hill and made my way back to CP hill. I remember that the day after we had returned to the hill, TB flags started popping up all over the place. Down toward the left were several compounds leading to a village area. There was a portion of the wadi that was used as a road way. It came from behind the hills and down to our left toward the wadi. It passed several buildings and a Mosque down closer to where the wadi and road met. The Mosque was flying TB colors. So, Marines started patrolling the surrounding area and tried to flush em out. Local village traffic had picked up, in between the fighting, and a van full of women and children hit an IED close to the Mosque. I guess the fuckers were back tracking and laying down IED's where they had seen us patrolling. It was a common tactic they used. Well, being the loving Americans that we are, we rallied up and went to the rescue of the people that had been blown up in the van. We humped the 700 yards to where the blast had hit. Children screaming, blood everywhere, moms crying, and men running around. We did what we could and called for a bird to transport the more serious wounded. It was so hot that day. I mean 'hot' - hot. The heat engulfed us as we treated the wounded. As we got the people separated and ready to transport, BANG! All hell broke loose! Those fuckers had set up an ambush on their own people in order to suck us in. They knew we would try and help. They were just waiting for us to get there. Rounds were flying by my head and then an AGL cut loose on us. The locals disappeared, and we were left with the wounded in the middle of a shit storm. Marines started dropping targets and calling out for ammo. It was a steady flow of lead in both directions. I reloaded a couple of times, after dropping some shitheads who were looking over a wall and firing their AK's from the hip. Idiots! I looked down and saw that I had spent five of my eight mags that I carried in my chest rig. Damn! Ammo was getting scarce. Lance had come with us to help the injured. I looked over and saw him pointing out targets and engaging. The fight grew into a crescendo of fire. It was like being in a huge hornet's nest. But, some of these hornets were glowing green and trying to sting me to death. The other Marines around me were 'focus-locked' on the enemy. I was lost in time for a moment. I got back in the fight and tried to do my part. I remember seeing a white truck moving behind the Taliban position. In the back of the truck was that damn AGL, spitting out grenades faster than a whore getting laid on pay day. We had the birds on station to transport the wounded locals, but they couldn't land in a hot zone. We kept on fighting and holding our ground. I reached to reload. No more mags! I grabbed a Marine next to me and asked for a mag. He complied and handed me another one. I got back up, scanning for the next shithead in my sights. As I was pulling slack on a Talib, I was knocked back by a blast from a grenade. Don't know if it was a 30mm from the AGL or a hand tossed one. Shit! I hoped they weren't that close. My bell was rung and I just sat there counting stars. A Marine kicked me in the leg and slapped my helmet. I spun around and shook off the clouds in my head. The white truck was gone, and the fight was dwindling. I suppose that the grenade was a last goodbye for the day. The TB packed their shit and moved out. We finally got the birds down and the wounded loaded. I helped load one of the little bitty girls that had been hit in the original blast. Poor baby was hurting and bleeding from her head. I talked to her in my redneck language and tried to calm her. We got them all on the HELO and we prepared to get back to the CP. We trudged our way back and finally made it. I sat down, poured a bottle of water over my head, and just sat there. I grabbed another bottle and slowly drank it down. The sun was setting down over the mountains, when I realized that we had been fighting for over nine hours down by the Mosque. I was pissed off. Those sons a bitches killed their own people just to get to us. The next day, Marines went hunting by the Mosque. They were on a joint patrol with ANA/ANP and made their way down the hill towards the Mosque area. One of the Marine SGTs, Paul Methvin, had an

ANA soldier go into the Mosque to see if it was being used for prayer or a den of iniquity. Guess what? Wasn't any praying going on there son! Not no, but hell no! It was a damn IED factory. The radio lit up, as the Marines were calling for me and EOD to get our asses down to the Mosque. I grabbed Blakey and another Marine, then headed toward the spot. EOD was downrange and it would be hours before they could arrive. We made our way down and around to the back side of the Mosque. On the inside of the main portion of the Mosque, no prayer signs or Qurans were present. No Imam, Mullah, or no one praying - no nothing. Attached to the backside of the building were two adjoining rooms. As I approached the Marines at the Mosque, I asked for a sit-rep. They ran the lick down to me and told me they had found some weapons and HME in the adjoining rooms. No shit? I dropped my bag and entered the first room. Holy Virgin Mary! It was the motherlode. The small room was packed floor to ceiling with every type of bomb making material you could think of. It was a terrorist's wet dream. It was dark and I had to use my flashlight to see my way around. I made a quick assessment, making sure it wasn't rigged to blow, and pulled out. Once I was back outside, I had a quick school circle with the Marines and got a plan together. They had set up a security perimeter. I had three or four other Marines make a daisy chain from the door of the cache location to a dug out area on the outside wall of the Mosque. My plan was to retrieve the HME and other goodies, then hand them off one at a time to the Marines outside. I told them to separate them by groups, so I could inventory all the evidence by type. Once we had our team set to begin, I re-entered the room. I had taken my PPE off, so I could move around a little better and to help with the heat. The room was a mud structure with no air flow or windows, just the entry door. I located a box with hundreds of homemade blasting caps. They were just like the ones I had found with LT Kay. They were wrapped in raw cotton and dipped in motor oil. I guess the Taliban had learned not to blow off their fingers from static electricity. There was shovels and templates for tubes and pressure plates. 20-30 pressure plates were ready made with wire, carbon rods, and plastic. Hundred pound bags of aluminum shavings were stacked in the corner, ready to be used for ANAL bombs. That's Ammonium Nitrate and Aluminum, not your anus! The aluminum is an oxidizer and gives the blast more bang for the buck. As I kept pulling out more and more shit, more shit appeared. There were Bulgarian anti-tank mines, RPG and Mortar propellant charge bags, Enfield and AK rifles with ammo, and on and on it went. I started to notice that every time I took a step, the floor would crackle and pop. What the hell? In one corner was a mud shelf built into the wall. On that shelf, I found a large wire screen that had been fastened to a wooden frame. It had a powder residue on the screen. It was being used as a large sifter. I looked closer and saw several small jars containing the powder. As I continued to move around and search, the damn floor continued to spark and pop. What the hell? I looked at the residue on the sifter, then got down on my hands and knees to the floor. Using my flashlight, I looked back and forth from the sifter to the dust on the floor. It looked and felt the same. What was it? I went back to the shelf and took a closer look. I saw some acetone bottles, cutting agents, hydrogen peroxide, - PEROXIDE! All stop, now! Shit! Shit! Shit! I was standing in a confined space full of every known HME in the terrorist world and PETN. The damn dust was PETN! The PETN was why it was popping and crackling every time I took a step. Ok, dumbass, what now? I grabbed some more items and carefully made my way outside. I called over to the Marines and gave them the skinny. I grabbed a radio and called up to CPT Calvin. I gave him a quick low down and waited for a response. Apparently, the fact that a civilian advisor was in a Mosque in Afghanistan, collecting bomb making materials, and that same civilian was fixing to reduce these items to dust, was a big deal. After a few minutes, some Ass-hat from way up the chain of command got on the horn and wanted a detailed sit-rep from me. I repeated my earlier report and stood by. Ass-hat came back and advised that we should just do a wash down of the location and collect what evidence we could. Oh Really! First off, where in the hell was I gonna get the five to six hundred gallons of water to do that. Secondly, Ass-hat had apparently never heard of a hypergolic reaction. A hypergolic reaction is when two substances ($H2O +?$) react spontaneously with an oxidizer (Peroxide) and causes an exothermic reaction. In other words, if I added water to the PETN, we would all be blown to shit. So, I kindly told Ass-hat "that was a no-go". I would continue to recover and collect the items for evidence and destruction. Thank you very much! We were not going to leave any of this shit for the bad guys to use against us. I finally got the room emptied with the help of the Marines. We had placed all the items in groups outside the Mosque. I took detailed photographs and notes for my report. All told, we had recovered approximately 800 lbs of explosives. It was a mixed bag of military grade munitions and HME. We had seized PETN, ANFO, HME, blasting caps, Pakistani det-cord, land mines, aluminum, and shovels, pick axes, templates, rifles, ammo, mortar rounds, and homemade land mines. It was unbelievable! It was a good hit and I know the sneaky bastards were pissed. Good! Get pissed! Come on down and we can talk about it! The time was dragging and EOD finally made it to the Mosque. The Gunny from EOD looked at our stash and was happily surprised. Being the explosive expert, he made his assessment and agreed that we had hit a good one. I collected what evidence I could carry, while the Gunny and the other Marines prepped the stuff to blow. Just when you think the stars had aligned and all was good - negative. We had done some good by finding the explosives and denying them to the TB. Guess who showed up, being nosy and acting like we were flogging Allah at the Mosque? You guessed it! The sneaky fuckers and that damn white truck with the AGL in the back. By this time, that damn white truck was my nemesis! I didn't know when or how, but his ass was mine. We started taking rounds and sporadic SAF from the front of the wadi. The Marines split into two groups and started bounding to the back of the Mosque. We cleared the Mosque and took cover behind a short 3 ft. wall. I can remember it like it was yesterday. You know the scene in "300", where one Spartan turns to another Spartan and says: "It is a good day to die" and "It would be a glorious death?" They were all smiles and laughing! I was on one knee taking cover with Marines on either side of me. We were all laughing like we had been smoking that Marijuana we were surrounded by. We couldn't help it! I turned to one Marine and asked how old he was. He responded, "19 Sir!" I turned to the other and asked the same. He said, "18 Sir!" All I could do was keep smiling. I continued to wonder how in the hell I had wound up in freaking Afghanistan, getting shot at by a Russian grenade launcher from the back of a Taliban truck, while trying to blow up a Mosque. It was a beautiful thing. The Gunny called out, "Fire in the hole!" We got tight and hunkered down behind our little wall. The blast took my breath away. The blast wave rushed over us in a flash, then the rocks and dust. The secondary effects of the bad guy explosives were devastating on the structural integrity of the Mosque. It caught fire. The wall and corner closest to the blast had collapsed. Sorry fuckers! No hard feelings! Quit using a house of worship for terror and maybe your shit won't get blown up! After the blast, the Taliban went ghost and disappeared into the village. We grabbed our shit and hustled back to CP hill. I really didn't hustle! I was hurting and tired. I had somehow hurt my back when I was running and dodging bullets. I kept my mouth shut and gritted my teeth to tough it out. The hump back was uneventful. We stayed quiet and I kept putting one foot in front of the other. The last 100 yards was hell for me. I looked and the other Marines were straining as well. The last portion was up hill and full of loose gravel and rocks. I slipped and fell forward, almost busting my face. Blakey helped me to my feet and asked if I was ok. I told him I was good to go and we continued. As the sun was setting, we made it to the top. I dropped my gear and peeled off my vest. Damn! I could finally get some rest! The evidence and my report would just have to wait till tomorrow. But little did I know, that the day was far from over. "Stand-to boys, guns out!

CHAPTER 19

Let me give you a hand...

———

JUST AS I PLOPPED MY tired ass down, a barrage of enemy RPG's started raining down on CP hill. Machine gun fire and tracers were bouncing all around. I was in between Lance's med truck and the command vehicle. Grabbing my vest and rifle, I made my way to the front of the hill, where we had fighting positions dug in. All the Marines, and I mean all of them, were setting up and preparing to defend the hill. We only had a small element of Marines for security. All the gun fighters were down range chasing their own Taliban. We had Lance and one of his Corpsman, Doc Jesse Reed, me and Ahern, CPT Calvin, the FAC Marine CPT, a radio operator, and a few Marines who were on the heavy guns and a MK19. Probably 10-12 of us against a shitload of unseen TB. We traced the fire back to the POO as best we could. The fire fight went back and forth for the next few hours. Every time we thought it was over, another RPG or mortar would splash down in front of or behind us. Then, more SAF would bounce around us. Eventually, the battle came to a stopping point. But, the fuckers kept taking pot shots at us throughout the night. At about zero dark thirty, we re-grouped at the command vehicle. 1st Sgt Ahern took a head and ammo count. Calvin, his radio operator, and the FAC stayed steady on the horn. I believe the FAC was CPT Paul Eckert, a really good guy and down to earth. He was a Cobra pilot if I recall, and a valuable asset to have on the ground. Just being able to talk to pilots and give them the info from another pilot's perspective was money. Hope you are well Paul, I miss hearing you fart in your sleep. It let me know that all was quiet on the radio, and Eeyore was resting. They had one Marine for security. Lance had his truck and Doc Jesse. That left me and Ahern with about six to eight other

Marines to defend our position. Steve placed Marines on the .50 and 240 in the dugout fighting positions on the outer edge of the hill. He turned back to me and asked, "Hey Old man, can you still work a .50?" What was I supposed to say? Steve told me his plan in detail. He handed me two smoke grenades and a red star cluster flare. He had the same. He told me he was getting on the gun in his truck and I would be in the other truck with the .50 cal. If shit got crazy, or the gunner went down, I should get on the gun if needed or if we got over run. He would pop smoke and a flare to signal. I was to do the same if I was out matched on my side. OK? This is when the shit got real! We shook hands and looked each other in the eye. Well, I tried to look him in the eye. I'm a foot shorter than Steve. So, I tippy-toed up and grabbed his shoulder. We gave each other the look and turned to go back towards our truck. As I was walking back to my truck, I heard Steve say, "Welcome to the Cone of Jackassery!" I got to my truck and crawled up inside. I hadn't touched a Ma-Deuce in years, and was scared to death about the timing and head space. Hopefully, I wouldn't have to test my skills. I just prayed that the last Marine that worked this gun knew what the hell he was doing. I didn't want to find out the hard way, in the dark while getting shot at. We stood our ground and waited. Sporadic fire was seen throughout the night, and radio traffic kept us informed of enemy movement. We kept waiting and waiting. I was going crazy sitting there. Every rock, tree, hill, or bush looked like a pack of hashish crazed Taliban running toward me. The damn NOD's I had would never focus enough for me to see clearly. The depth perception was shit. After what seemed like a lifetime, I could see the sun coming up behind us. Maybe the fuckers went home to sleep? Wrong again! One of the Marine units, down past the wadi between Ortiz hill and the ridge, came under heavy machine gun and RPG fire. The Marines were stuck between bullets and bombs, and needed CAS fast. Air got on station and starting blasting the AO with a show of force, while trying to flush out the bad guys. It seemed like all of our TB from the CP hill attack had pushed out and regrouped further down from the wadi where the Marines were at. Ahern pulled us down from our fighting positions and we maintained a somewhat normal security posture. One of the Talibs, who was shooting at the Marines down range, thought it would be a good idea to try and shoot down one of the planes with his machine gun or some stupid shit like that. What a dumbass! All I know is hit got lit up with an airborne delivery explosive. The pilot got PID on his location and cut loose with a bomb, or JDAM, or some type of damn munition. I can't remember what type. The firing stopped and no more Taliban were seen. LTC Tipton and Sgt Major Black had pushed out and were rolling around the AO. They wanted a BDA of the strike. I loaded up in a truck and made it to the area of the dead Taliban. Next to a qualat under a tree, I saw about two feet of intestines and a shoe. Up in the tree was a shawl and a turban that apparently had been blown up there during the blast. A large puddle of blood was on the ground, and a portion of a human torso was thrown about 20 meters past the tree. SGT Ken Rick and his crew had been posted up in the wadi, just waiting to get shot at, so they could kill fuckers and pick their brains. Rick was tasked to do the BDA and help me out. I hooked up with SGT Rick and asked what the hell happened. He ran it down to me and pointed to the different areas the TB had been shooting from. Then, he pointed to the Turban tree and explained what the dumbass was doing before he was blown into pieces. We all knew that we had a pretty extensive IED builder or builders in the area. So, I was always getting fingerprints or DNA from either dead or captured Taliban. I was trying to get an affirmative link to a bad guy from the area, showing a pattern or location he was operating in. Sgt. Rick, myself, and another Marine spread out. We started looking for any evidence I could collect and push up to be analyzed. I stood under the Turban tree and scanned the area. We got on line and starting walking, while checking our 5's and 25's. About twenty yards from the tree, I located a hand that had been blown off of dumbass. I reached into my drop pouch and grabbed a pair of latex gloves. I put them on and picked up the hand. As I stood up, the skin around the hand fell off like it was tissue paper. Damn! No getting fingerprints! I carried the hand over to the tree and pulled out a cotton swab to get DNA. As I was finishing up, Rick called out that he had found the other hand. I went over to where he was standing and looked down at his feet. Sure enough! There was dumbass' hand number two. It was intact and had about three inches above the wrist still attached. It was burnt and grimy. I picked up the hand and carried it over to a small irrigation canal. Rick and the other Marine came over to help. I grabbed my back pack and pulled out my gear. A camera, more gloves, fingerprint kit, paper evidence bag, sharpie pen, and my notebook. I photographed the hand, then grabbed another couple of cotton swabs. I swabbed the open area of the wrist to get a good blood sample. Then, I set them aside. I looked at the fingertips and saw they were covered in grease and grim. I asked if anybody had some hand sanitizer. Rick looked at me like I was asking for a beer and a hot dog. The other Marine reached into his cargo pocket and pulled out a small plastic bottle of sanitizer. I thanked him and took it. I grabbed the hand and covered it with the sanitizer. I then walked over to the irrigation canal and proceeded to wash the hand in between my hands, as if I was getting ready to eat dinner. The Marines just gawked at me and shook their heads. Rick said he had never seen any shit like that before. I finished washing the hand and then told Rick to, "Give me a hand." Pun intended! I broke out my trusty baby wipes, which I had stashed in a Ziploc from my right cargo pocket. Back home, the baby wipes are used for when we take prints on AFIS. The oils in the baby wipe towel help bring out the prints. I dried the hand, rubbed the baby wipe over each finger, then the thumb. The hand got pretty clean and I was able to clearly see the ridges and groves of the fingertips. I had Rick hold the print card and ink pad, while I inked up the fingertips. I rolled out each finger, then thumb, and finally a four finger print onto the card. I must say it was the easiest fingerprint I have ever taken in my whole career. There was no arm to get in the way and no one trying to pull back. About this time, the Boss and Sgt Maj arrived on scene. They asked for a SIT-REP and Sgt Rick filled them in while I finished up. I put the print card and the SD card with photos into a manila envelope. I scrawled a quick field note card, of where, when, and how? Then, I placed it into the same envelope. I then put the swabs in a different one and sealed both envelopes. Sometime during the course of processing the hand, it appeared as if it was 'shooting the finger'. Maybe a pic was taken, I don't know who took it, or who that that hand belonged to! So, don't ask! I put the hand into another larger evidence bag and marked it. I gathered up my gear, before putting the hand and other evidence into my bag. All of a sudden, we heard enemy fire again. It was pretty close, but I never got a good POO on the bad guys. Maybe they were pissed because I was taking dumbasses' hand? I don't know the real reason why, but the Boss was foot patrolling the area, looking at the aftermath of the bomb, and doing his own

BDA. The fuckers were trying to get lucky I guess. LTC Tipton had pushed out and behind the qualat, where we couldn't see him. OH SHIT! I grabbed my rifle and took cover behind the qualat under the Turban tree. Sgt Maj Black, myself, Sgt Rick, and a LCPL started bounding and clearing to the next building in order to get eyes on the LTC. SGTMAJ Black kicked in a metal door to a gate leading to a courtyard. Holy shit Batman! I was doing CQB tactics in fucking Afghanistan with the BN SGTMAJ, and other MARINES, moving to cover down on the BN CO. It was surreal, to say the least. I button hooked through the gate and posted up on the right angle of the courtyard. We pushed up another 30 yards or so through the compound, and out the back entrance leading to an open farm field flanked by a tree line. I saw LTC Tipton on the edge of the field. He was looking around like he was planning D-Day or how in the hell he was going to use his Marines to kill the sneaky fuckers. Hell! I don't know what he was doing, but he was the Boss. What the hell was I going to tell him? SGTMAJ ran out to him and they exchanged words. LTC Tipton nodded, then they casually walked back to us. We re-grouped and headed back, when some Jump Marines rushed over. They escorted the LTC and SGTMAJ back toward the edge of the wadi, where their trucks were parked. I say escorted, but the Boss went and did whatever the hell he wanted, or what he thought he had to do, to help his Marines kill. Black looked at me with a smirk, then shook his head. I kinda shrugged back and gave him an, "I don't know" look. They cleared out and moved on to whatever the hell command guys do. I got my trash and looked for my truck to take me back to CP hill. I had been up for 50-60 hours non-stop, and I was feeling it. When I got back to the hill, I told Calvin I had to get 'the hand' on a bird to the lab at KAF. We had a re-supply coming in the next day. So, I could get it on that flight. I dropped my gear, made it over to Lance's truck, and sat down. I was in so much pain from the previous day, when I had hurt my back. I didn't want Calvin or Ahern to know about it. I was scared they would send my ass to the rear. I told Lance what was up and he checked me out. No place for rehab or treatment. He broke out an IV and hooked me up. Then he gave me a shot of Toradol in the IV. I almost passed out! I was on cloud nine instantly. Lance told me to drink some water and he handed me a bottle. The pain was gone and I was starting to doze off. After the IV had finished, Lance told me to stay close because he wanted to monitor any effects of the pain killer. I grabbed my sleeping gear, then crawled into his truck to sleep. Lance checked on me throughout the night and I had the best sleep I had gotten since being in Kablamistan. The next morning, I was feeling much better. I grabbed my little stove and made a big batch of hot coffee. I poured some for Lance and thanked him. He shook it off with his, "Just doing my job Bro" attitude. I saw the bird coming over the hills. I grabbed 'the hand' and other evidence for transport. I ran out to the HELO and spoke with the pilot by headset. He asked what it was. So, I told him. He didn't want to touch it and pointed to the deck of the bird. I saw an empty MRE box and placed it in there. I turned to the crew chief and grabbed his shoulder. Over the headset, I told him it was evidence and where it needed to go. He gave me a thumbs up. Then, I jumped down and headed back to the hill. I looked back as the bird was lifting off and saluted the pilot. He gave me the finger and smiled! Just another day in the life of LEP ACTUAL with 3/7. The fun never stops! No really! It didn't stop, just keep reading!

CHAPTER 20

Hell or Sangin, it's all the same to me

———

OUR TIME IN MUSA QUALA had come to an end. We killed a lot of Taliban but paid a price for it. Bailey, Cueto and Patino were all good men that did their duty and what they thought was right. No matter how many bad guys we killed, nothing could replace the loss of these men. War is hell! Sacrifices must be made, and I know the Boss felt their loss as much as each Marine did. We were moving out to the next terrorist vacation spot. A place called Sangin. Sangin was a Taliban stronghold in Helmond Province. The Brits had been fighting there as a Coalition ally for the past seven years or so. They had lost some good men over the years, and they seemed to be losing ground. The Brits were good soldiers, but their government just never really gave them the support they needed to close with and destroy the enemy. Hell, close with and smash the enemy was just what Marines do. They had several small PB's and FOB's scattered about the AO. FOB's Jackson, Inkerman and Nolay were the places we would be operating from. The goal was to find and kill the TB where they called home. The Taliban ran freely throughout the area and had never been met with an overwhelming in your face onslaught. Kilo and Wpns would push out from Inkerman and make their way to the river approximately 2-3 klicks away. This section of territory was full of TB like ticks on a hound. India and additional Wpns Co Marines would operate out of Nolay and Lima would move out from Jackson. I wound up at Inkerman with Kilo Company and Josh and his boys. Lt's Dzierzak, Birchum, and Goodwin were there. All good men and ready to keep fighting and killing. But the man that stood out was CPT Ryan Cohen. Kilo 6! Here was a man that was born a Marine. His daddy was a Marine and he grew up in a Marine household. I don't think there ever was a doubt about his destiny. Cohen arrived to 3/7 right before we deployed and I never had the chance to hit it off with him before we got to Afghanistan. By the time we had pushed to Inkerman, it was obvious that his men loved him and would follow him into hell with their hair on fire and drinking jet fuel! His quick thinking and steady push to smash the enemy is legend in Kilo Company lore. I got stuck at the FOB on the first day of the push for Kilo. I think that they didn't want the old guy to catch one in the face while they were busy killing bad guys. It was a kick in the ass for the Marines, and they suffered several Marine WIA's, and a bunch of enemy KIA during the battle. Command had been told by the Brits that they had never gotten as far as the river, and doubted we would. It was a running joke from the Brits, that we wouldn't make and they would see us in time for "tea" that evening. Obviously they didn't understand how Marines operate or how we relish killing. Cohen deployed engineers with MICLIC's and APOBS to blow their way to the river. These were mine defeating charges that cleared a path of destruction by exploding any existing IED's that were in the way. Talk about destroy! The APOBS were man portable and cleared a 45-meter foot trail in its wake. But the big boy was the MICLIC! It was on a tank frame with a small barrel sticking out. It would send a rocket attached to a long line of explosives about 100 meters ahead. On impact it would clear out a path 8-10 meters wide and 100 meters long. It was impressive and scared the hell out of the Taliban. My buddy, Ranson Martel, was a Kilo Marine, and a man I would come to love and mentor after his time in the Corps. He is a Deputy Sheriff and a sniper with the SWAT team now. I am proud of him and glad he is still a part of my life. On the second day I was able to get down range with Kilo and start collecting evidence for TSE. I hooked up with Ransom and he filled me in on what kinda shit they had been dealing with. He told me how they had pushed up to within 400-500 yards from a compound that was turned into PB Fires. The Taliban had been using the compound as a field hospital, and thought they would never be hit there. As Kilo approached, they were taking fire from all sides, but it was ineffective. Cohen called up a MICLIC and fired that bitch off. Ranson said it sounded like they had launched a space shuttle. It shot out over a tree line and made a huge explosion. Almost immediately TB radio traffic was asking, "What the fuck was that?" The Talibs shit their pants and pulled back, fleeing the compound hospital with their wounded, leaving supplies and bloody rags and ammo. Then the enemy radio was telling other Taliban that they had shot down a plane, and that the explosion was the plane hitting the earth. That's some funny shit right there! Kilo 1st PLT took that compound and turned it into PB Fires. They would continue to operate out of Fires for the remaining deployment in Sangin. Fires became famous for the "Stoned goat called PePe". That damn goat kept eating the Marijuana surrounding Fires, and would wander in and out, stumbling around the compound. As well, as the mouse catching cat named, "Tiger". I have also been assured that none of the Kilo 1 Marines ever utilized the garden and peach orchard to make any homebrew "Hooch". That tale is just a figment of someone's imagination! (Wink Wink) I know my buddy Jacob Fry was there, as well as Colon, Birchum, Dinsmore, Levi Unzeitig, (love that name, Levi) and Patterson. Baby Ando's ass was also in the mix with them. With his smart assed commentary that had me rolling. Cohen rallied the men and kept pushing further toward the river after Fires was secured. PB's Dragon, Bulldog and Helmond would result in being established after three days of constant in your face fighting. Enemy positions fired upon the Marines from distances as far as 200 meters, and as close as 5 meters. CPT Cohen would earn a Silver Star for his actions during the day's long fight. He led his men from the front, and gave them the push they needed to continue the fight. His leadership style is the hallmark of a Marine Infantry Officer. I am blessed to say he has become a dear friend and a man I can turn to for anything. Ryan, thank you for supporting me and taking care of me while I was under your care. I know I was a pain in the ass at times, but you pushed me in the way I could help your Marines, and I am grateful for the experience. I met up with Josh and Patsy and all the old crew from Musa Quala. It was like a reunion. Blakey and Wooly Bully where there, and the fun had really just started. After the PB's had been established, I was sequestered to PB Bulldog, where Cohen had sat up his CP. About two-three hundred yards away was PB Helmond, right on the river, and with its own canal running behind its back entrance. I got into a groove and helped out the best way I could. I still had my trusty bean pot and big tea kettle. I looked like a traveling Gypsy, with all the shit I managed to carry around. Making coffee in the mornings, and hot chow in the evenings from the large sized precooked meals. They were platoon sized MRE's, and tasted like shit. I would combine the meals and add some seasoning the best I could. Josh would help when he wasn't out patrolling, and eventually it became a daily ritual to see what Ronnie could come up with. Do you remember seeing old WWII Marines in black and white photos with a cigarette hanging from their lip, and barking orders or killing? We had a Marine Sgt that should have been around in that time. Camden MacGregor was a guy that was hard not to like. Tough and a voice that sounded like he gargled with rocks, and rinsed with gravel. He always had a cigarette in his mouth. Or one behind his ear, one in his mouth, one in his hand, and reaching for one in his pack. That damn guy could out smoke a chimney. Mac was one of the SGT's leading Marines when they had been inserted by HELO. We made fast friends and we passed the time between patrols and guard duty playing cards and bullshitting. He is another lead from my example NCO's that the Marine Corps is lucky to have. Jeff Mahaffey was also there and added his usual wit to the mix. Pretty boy Shane Otwell was another Marine that was always in the mix, and his attitude was contagious. Shane was a blast to be around and he was another country boy from Arkansas. Then along comes Gunny Hussey. Now Gunner Hussey. Jimmy Hussey is a knife handing, in your face, do what the hell I say type guy, that knows no quit or any other way that doesn't mean smashing bad guys in the face. I had a hard time getting close to him at first, but he is as soft on the inside as he is hard on the outside. Like a bull headed Marine leader should be. He was and still is. Like all the command that was with 3/7, they were hard, and did what it took to get the job done, but they cared for every Marine around them. That is no BS, you can see it in the way 3/7 Marines still reach out to one another up and down the chain of command to this very day. Jimmy was always pushing and pulling Marines to their limits. They didn't always like it, but the results were clear. Days passed, and I got into a routine of going out on patrol as much as I could, but usually I had to sort whatever evidence was brought to me from the Marines in the field. The Taliban were always probing the different PB's with RPG's and machine gun fire. We would push out and try to maneuver against them and kill em as we found em. They would try to sneak up as close as they could and toss grenades over the wall of our compound and trigger a fight. Most times they got punched in the chest with rifle fire. On one of these occasions we got PID on a group of TB trying to push up on Bulldog. Hussey grabbed his rifle and charged out the exit and starting bounding toward the enemy. I was next to him and didn't see any Marines follow. I did what came natural. I grabbed my shit and ran after Jimmy. We got about 200 yards outside our compound when he stopped and turned toward me. Not knowing that it was just me, he started rattling off instructions and calling for a radio, thinking he was talking to a bunch of Marines. He finally realized it was me, and asked me, "What the fuck are you doing old man?" I shrugged and told him I wasn't going to let him have all the fun by himself. I believe at that moment there, I earned his respect. I wasn't just some nasty civilian he had to look after. We had ended up deep in a corn field, with the Taliban up on a small two or three-foot ridge by a canal, sixty or so yards away. 3-4 Marines finally made it our way, along with 2-3 ANA soldiers. Gunny got on the radio, relayed some info and then split us into two groups. I wound up with one Marine and one ANA soldier in my group. Thanks Jimmy! Gunny took the rest of the men and said he was going to flank the Taliban positions. WPNS trucks would be moving up from the other side. The TB were dug into what we called, "Murder Holes". Reinforced mud and wood fighting positions. A few minutes passed and the corn above my head started falling from the bullets cutting through the air above me. I fell onto my back and started praying. I looked over at the Marine with me, and he was doing the same. The damn ANA soldier was still standing there grinning and pointing toward the enemy firing positions. I motioned for him to get down. He finally got down and shrugged his shoulders at me. Me and the Marine rolled over into a prone and motioned to the ANA. We pointed to the TB position and held up our rifles. He nodded and we got ready to en- gage. I could hear Gunny and his boys shooting and the enemy fire shifted from us to them. I held up my hand showing three fingers to the Marine with me and started counting off. As my third finger dropped, we started shooting at the bad guys. I emptied a mag and began a reload. I looked at the ANA soldier and he was just lying there watching us. What the hell? I pointed at his rifle and then the area of the TB. He nodded again and I continued to reload and got back in the fight. I finally heard the distinct sound of AK fire going out instead of coming in. The ANA was spraying and praying, but at least it was a little suppressive fire for us. CAAT trucks moved in and got the big guns into play, and the fight was over as fast as it started. I grabbed my gear and by the time I made it to the Murder Holes, the area was cleared. I did my TSE thing, and we pushed back to Bulldog. Once inside, Jimmy pulled me off to the side and scolded me in private. Not in the Gunny Hussey knife hand way, but it was I appreciate your help, but don't scare me like that again type of way. From then on it wasn't Gunny Hussey, it was Jimmy. Jimmy is my friend and I was so glad to see him a few months ago before he re-deployed to another Marine assignment as a Gunner. Love you brother, you make me proud to be a Marine! My time at Bulldog was extended, and I would eventually make my way around to the different PB's as needed. The reality of it all became a cluster of days and nights of Taliban sneaky fucker tactics and Marines continuing to close with, engage, and kill the enemy by whatever means available. I was witness to every day Heroics by the men around me. My time with Kilo and Ryan Cohen is a part of my every day existence. I have daily or weekly contact with men that I shared so many experiences with while I was there. You all are a part of me, and part of the reason I am writing this book. Kilo, take that hill! Breathe Fire!

CHAPTER 21

Gunner...The Man..The Myth.The Legend!

———

CHIEF WARRANT OFFICER 4 MATTHEW Carpenter, Gunner Carpenter, Matt Carpenter, or just plain Gunner! *The USMC MOS 0306 is referred to as "The Gunner". Gunners are weapons specialists and are experts in the tactical deployment of all infantry weapons in the Marine Corps arsenal. The requirements to be a Gunner are stringent, and much higher than what is needed for other Warrant Officer appointments. Gunners are not appointed, but commissioned, and are authorized to wear the "Bursting Bomb" insignia. * (Excerpt from Marine Corps Times online) Matt was a legend in 3/7 and had been deployed several times in Iraq and now in Afghanistan. He had worked his way up and been given responsibilities of command as a SSGT and a Gunny. I believe I heard that he had spent time in the 7th Marines from CPL to Gunner. His actions in Iraq were already told around the camp fire. Matt was a proven leader and a wealth of tactical knowledge. Being from rural Pennsylvania, Matt was a tough guy and a true patriot. I could see he cared about every Marine under his influence, and pushed his skills down to the lowest level. Every Infantry Marine knows that no one messes with the Gunner in whatever Battalion they are in. That was also the case in 3/7! Gunner had his own crew and he went wherever the hell he wanted, or where he thought he could best advise the Boss and kill the enemy. We had met back at 29 Palms and became friends. We even traced our Marine lineage back to the 8th Marines at LeJeune, when we were both snot nosed LCPL's. That meant he was "Old School" and a "Salty-assed" Marine. One of his crew, or an "Assistant Gunner" was SGT Philip Noble. Noble was a Texas boy from Corsicana in north-east Texas. Being Texas boys, we hit it off and smoked and joked about home and other things guys from Texas bullshit about when away from home. Philip was a hard charger and always on the move with Gunner and off to wherever he was told. The Taliban continued to use their sneaky fucker tactics up and down the AO from Fires to Helmond PB's using the "Cohen Expressway". The Cohen Expressway was the route that CPT Cohen had blown from Inkerman to the river using the APOBS and MICLIC's. Shadow was called up and had gotten with CPT Cohen to make a plan of attack. I listened to the order and was impressed with how they were to be deployed. After the head shed, I turned to Ryan and told him I should go out with the snipers to get evidence from whatever guys they killed. Maybe I could snatch a finger print or DNA swab that was a match in the system. Ryan thought about two seconds and shook his head no. Shit, what the hell, I tried! I guess Ryan thought I was crazy for wanting to go out with the boys. I know I was old and slow, but I still wanted to do my part. I was going stir crazy being stuck at Bulldog day in and day out. Our FAC was a Marine pilot called "Mickey". He was a smart guy and always had a smile on his face and never got excited about anything. Mickey and I got along well, and spent many hours monitoring the radios together whenever I was stuck at the PB. Hey Mick, I'm still waiting on you for the beer run! Shadow pushed out at dark and set up where they knew TB were moving in and out of the area. I was on my rubber bitch trying to fall asleep, and counting the stars. Blakey, Wooly Bully, Josh, and Patsy where there to support with their CAAT trucks. I got to sleep and tossed and turned my way to whatever I was dreaming of. The compound we were in was surrounded by corn and Marijuana fields. We had goats and rats running in and out of the place. One of the goats was a baby and weighed about twenty pounds. I kept hearing Blakey and some of the Marines scheming and talking about getting that goat into my bean pot for chow. I woke up and rolled over looking for my water bottle. What the hell? Standing over me was Blakey, with a rock that weighed about forty pounds, holding it over his head with both hands. At first I thought he had gone all PTSD and was gonna kill me! But standing under him was that baby goat. I yelled up to him and asked, "Blakey, what the hell are you doing?" He looked down at me and replied, "Shit Ronnie, I'm hungry!" Damn son, hang on a minute! I told him to set his big ass down and not to kill the goat. He complied and threw the rock down and then sat down next to me. I got the coffee going and found some chow to cook before Blakey starting skinning Marines and going all cannibal on us. Shadow was still out and waiting on the enemy to move. The morning turned into the ever present afternoon heat wave. I was just sitting at Bulldog, but I can imagine the shit Shadow was having to deal with. No sleep, chow, and just lying in wait. Just like it was planned, the TB finally started moving, and getting closer to where Shadow had set up. I still don't know if the bastards planned what happened next, or they were just lucky on the time and place. Unknown to Shadow, the Taliban had another hardened murder hole in the area. As the bad guys moved into range of the snipers, the TB had men in the fighting positions as well as in the surrounding compounds. Shadow took some shots and dropped several bad guys. The response was quick, and the whole area opened up with enemy machine guns and AK's. Shadow was penned down by fire and couldn't maneuver. They kept engaging targets and dropping shitheads as they appeared. But the TB started to flank out around them. I don't know why or how, but Gunner was across the river with his crew in a hasty over watch position. I think he was using his optics to get a clear view of what was happening and Gunner was putting the pieces in place. Gunner quickly reached out and got CAS on station. If I remember correctly, it was HELO gunships, Apaches I think. Gunner started relaying targets and calling out instructions and enemy movements. Back at Bulldog, we jumped up to provide a QRF, and headed toward the fight. I wound up in a CAAT truck with Blakey and his crew. We pushed back and around behind PB Bulldog through some 10ft high corn fields. The goat path we were on lead us right through the ever present Marijuana and corn fields. It was boggy and muddy. The truck was sliding and hopping all over the damn place. As we approached, the front end of the truck sunk into the ground, and we started rolling over on our right side. Man! What the shit? We wound up half-ass rolled over. I crawled my big ass out the back hatch while one of the Marines propped it open and pulled me out by my hand. Once on the ground, Blakey, me and the other Marines headed toward the fight. CPT Cohen had grabbed a group of Marines and was about 200 yards away in a parallel position headed in the same direction we were. But we didn't know that at the time. Blakey grabbed some reeds and grass to use as camo and starting putting it on his helmet and using mud on his face. Why not, seemed like a good idea to me, so I followed suit. We started back on track toward the fight when a large blast was heard and seen through the corn field. Afterward, we learned that CPT Cohen had snatched up a LAW or SMAW gunner and had him hit the bunker where the enemy were entrenched. This gave Shadow some relief and allowed them to get on the move to find more targets. HELO's were coming in and shooting rockets and then they opened up with that bad-ass chain gun hanging under their nose. Gunner was directing fire over the radio and all hell was breaking loose. The Taliban had come out of hiding and started firing back at Marine positions with full force. I don't know how many we killed, but it was a lot. I kept ducking and dodging through the corn and Marijuana fields with the other Marines. We never really got to engage from our vantage point, and only took well aimed shoots whenever we could see Taliban running for their lives after a gun run or rocket shot. I finally got to the edge of the river and we kinda hooked our way to the left, through some irrigation canals. We found some cover and find a good fighting spot. As we were moving, we heard someone call out on the radio about enemy movement at the river near the canal. Shit! That's close to us! We ran as fast as our gear would allow and got down behind a berm on the other side of the canal, and started looking for insurgents. I didn't see or hear any movement. WTF! Then the radio traffic said, "They are running to cover and just got down behind the canal!" Wait a second! That was us! Someone saw us through the fields and canal, and assumed we were the bad guys trying to maneuver on Marines. SHIT, SHIT, SHIT! Blakey had our radio guy roger up that it was us and not bad guys. But about that time one of the gunships came over head and started cutting loose with that damn machine cannon. Hot brass was falling all around us like giant hot glitter. It was unreal. Thank God he saw us! But apparently we hadn't seen the Taliban sneaking up to us from where we had been taking cover. Damn that was close. After that last big gun run from above, the gun fight volume turned down almost instantly. We got a head count of our guys and made our way back to our truck. We got another MRAP to pull up and we winched and strapped that heavy son of bitch for almost two hours trying to get it clear of the mud hole. After almost wanting to pull our hair out, the truck was clear. Muddy, but clear, the truck was ready to roll. Looking around we looked like a rag tag bunch of nasty bastards. Come to think of it, we were, and I knew I hadn't had a bath or shower the last month or so. It was getting so bad, you couldn't take a shit or unbutton your pants without smelling your own filth, even before you did your business. Finally, back at Bulldog, I found my spot and sat down. Pulled my boots off and put on my good old Mickey Mouse sandals. Grabbed my tea kettle and got some water hot. Marines started trickling in by squads and teams, looking tired and spent. It was a hell of a fight. But it had become just another everyday part of these Marines lives. Daily grind of patrol, shoot, and move and communicate. Close with and engage the enemy. Meet em head on or from the side or the rear. It didn't matter. These men were stretched thin and pushed to their physical limits. No sympathy to hand out though. Tough shit, do your job, we are all tired. So on it went, day in and day out with a new gun fight to fight, or IED to exploit, or mortar to dodge. Looking back, I am amazed that we didn't lose any more Marines. We were in a daily meat grinder from can to can't. I guess we didn't realize it at the time because we were too busy fighting and killing and trying to live. Shit, I don't know. I kept on making coffee in the mornings and chow in the evenings. I helped Mickey on the radios, and collected whatever evidence came my way. Some days was just plain boring. Some days were full of mortars and grenades, and getting shot at. We were a steady presence in the AO, and we denied the Taliban freedom of movement. They couldn't just jump on their motorcycle and go to Mohammed's house for ammo or tea, or some Man love anymore. Well, the fun continued, and the stories kept on coming. Have you ever seen a Sgt Maj get so mad, that one of his eyes looks like it's going to burst right out of his eye socket? I have, and it's not a pretty sight. Unless you are in the crowd just watching. Then it's pretty damn funny. Hang in there and I will tell you the story of a young Marine that stabbed a General, and the Sgt Maj wanting to kill him before he stroked out. It was all fun and games boys and girls.

CHAPTER 22

Go ahead Marine...stab the GENERAL!

———

THE TIME WENT BY AND the hits kept on coming. Hitting the enemy in the face with whatever weapon we had. The TB never really got face to face with us after the initial push anymore. They would use their sneaky fucker tactics, and probe us with grenades and RPG's. Whenever we could find them in the open, we would kill em. The only advantage they had was knowing the terrain, and using the corn and Marijuana fields for cover. Pretty soon we had their backyards mapped out and learned the different routes they used to sneak around. What 3/7 had accomplished up to that point was apparently a big deal at higher headquarters. The word was that General Mills was coming down range to mingle with the boys, and get a first-hand look at death and destruction. I settled into a routine, and was spitting out coffee every morning like a new Starbucks in Afghanistan. 1st SGT Mike Woods had replaced Krause after he had been hit at the potato from a mortar attack. I got up every morning and got my kettle boiling with water, brush my teeth, get a dip then my morning shit break. I would help Mickey with the radio and wait for the shit to start. If Marines had a known location to search, I would push out and gather what Intel or evidence I could. On one of these patrols, we had a compound that always had a lot of TB foot traffic in and out of it, before and after we would get hit with SAF or IDF. I jumped on a patrol and we pushed out to the target. Marines approached the qualat, and began looking for people to kill. One Marine was pushing up with a metal detector to clear a path. As he approached it got really quiet. UH-OH! Not good! Where are you, you fucker? The Marines got their heads on a swivel and spread out behind the clearance detector. As the Marine with the detector got to within 3-5 feet from the gate entrance of the qualat, BOOM! Another damn IED! We jumped and took cover, then started our buddy drills to get to the downed Marine and look for the ambush. No ambush happened. The downed Marine was lucky. The HME was a wet or bad charge, and only broke his foot or ankle. Maye not broken but hurt pretty good without the open wound from a normal IED. Damn that guy was lucky. We pushed on through the compound and cleared it for bad guys. No takers where found. The Marines were just aching to muzzle thump some Talibs. Lucky for them, they had pussed out and left the area. I got a couple of guys and started my TSE, while the other helped out Doc with treating the hurt Marine. I gathered up the remnants of the IED and processed the scene. We re-grouped and patrolled our way back to Bulldog. I met up with CPT Cohen and 1st SGT Woods and gave them an update. Since General Mills was coming out to visit, I thought I would do a story board of the IED and give him a visual of what was being used against us. I found a board and wire tied all the components of the IED down to the board. I then labeled them and drew a sketch of the compound and location of the IED. Now, the General was the commander of the 1st MEF and he had SGT MAJ Barrett as his lead enlisted man. They, along with COL Kennedy and his SGT MAJ, LTC Tipton and SGT MAJ Black were coming to see the Marines in the field. That my friends, is a lot of clout. We had the MEF, Regimental and Battalion bosses headed are way Needless to say, Marines were nervous and hoping to fly under the radar. The bosses made their way down the Cohen Expressway, stopping at the PB's along the way. Once they made it to Bulldog, the General meet with and greeted all the Marines, along with SGT MAJ Barrett. Ole Derek Hopkins and Brother Chuck were handing out MRE's to the boys trying to hurry up and get settled in. It was all good, but you could see Troy Black in the background knife handing and pointing out various tasks and instruction to Marines in the area. The General decided it was time for chow and wanted to eat an MRE with his Marines. A hasty school circle was called and all the junior Marines huddled up around the General to eat. The rest of the command element was posted up near the compound entrance just watching and listening. You could feel their eyes punching holes in you, daring you to fuck up. I know I was just a nasty civilian, but hell, it was the General. I was shaking inside and trying to figure out what to say when my time came to brief him. One poor Marine, LCPL Ryan Kinne, young and probably as nervous as the rest of us, jumped down in front of General Mills and began to open his MRE. General Mills began speaking and asking questions of the young Marines around him. Those damn MRE bags are really thick plastic rubber stuff that are hard to open by hand, and it was common practice to open one end of the bag with knife. What I saw next almost gave me a heart attack. It happened so fast, but in my mind it was like a car wreck in slow motion. You can see the impact coming, but you can't do anything to stop it. Kinne, while sitting in front of the General, reached into his pocket and pulled out a knife. He then casually began to cut open one end of the bag while he was looking up and trying to pay attention to what the General was saying. One corner of those bags kind of folds and get thicker at the edge. That knife must have been dull as my ass, because it stopped on the thick edge and hung up. I'm standing behind the General with my story board, and looking at the Kinne below him. The young Marine felt the blade stop, then tugged on the handle to pull it through. About the time the General had sat down and turned to get comfortable, Kinne was fighting the MRE. The knife made it through, and stopped in the General's leg. Holy Shit Marine, Choke Yourself! The General never flinched, he looked down, brushed it aside like it was no big deal and continued with his speech. General Mills made a quick joke about a Purple Heart while brushing his pants leg. I thought Troy Black and Gunny Hussey were gonna stroke out on the spot. The sudden rush of air from everyone sucking in, was like being in the twilight zone. I didn't know what to do. The laser eye shots coming from Troy, could have burned a hole into steel. This has to be the only time in Marine combat history that a Marine General has been stabbed on the battlefield while surrounded by Marines when the stabber didn't die. Kinne, you goofy son of a bitch! High Five! But, the General was a Marine, he continued to push and they all ate their MRE's. After chow, I got to show my story board and answer what questions the General asked of me. He thanked me and shook my hand. He was a really nice man and a pleasure to be around. You could tell he cared for his Marines and it showed. Before Kinne could get choked to death by Black or Hussy, the General decided he wanted to move on down to PB Helmond on the river. Instead of riding in his MRAP, he wanted to walk there. It was only 200-300 yards away, but shit this was still Indian Country, and getting a shot at the General would be a bad day for us. But what the hell? He is the General, who is going to tell him no. Marines got up and formed a security ring around him and began to push out to PB Helmond. The General and the rest of the command stayed close to each other and answered his questions while walking. Guess what? The TB happened to be in a fighting mood and started cutting loose with SAF all around the compound. I think Mahaffey was closest to the General and helped escort him to his truck. I know shit was flying everywhere and Marines were hustling to get on target and kill more bad guys. It was a quick affair and the Taliban didn't stay engaged long. The command element pushed out and it was back to the normal grind. I was really starting to stink and was tired of gaging on my own B.O. every time I dropped my drawers or changed my socks. We had a slit trench outside the back door that was about ten-foot-long, two-foot-wide and three to four foot deep. We blocked it with sand bags and used ammo boxes to shit from. Every time I had to shit, I had to get a dip and light a cigarette to try and keep from gagging on the smell of the trench and my own body odor. Then I would balance my fat ass on an ammo box, holding my rifle, watching mortars or rockets go over head, swatting at huge flies trying to fly up your ass while dropping a deuce. I was just waiting to get blown down or fall into the shit trench. That would have been my luck. Fuck this, I needed a bath! I heard that the Marines at PB Helmond were living the life of luxury by having their own day spa canal at the back door. I jumped on the next rotation patrol down to Helmond to get a bath and get a different view of the battlefield. When I got to Helmond, I saw that the compound was right on the river, and had a canal running directly behind the back entrance. The Marines had some ANA with them and they split the compound between them. Sgt. Rogers was there, and we hugged and kissed in the way that Marines do. I dropped my shit and skinned down to my silkies. I didn't have any soap, so I asked around, and a large bottle of shampoo appeared. I told Seth I was going to get in the canal and clean up. I eased down into the cool water and settled in. It felt so damn good, it had been weeks (56 days) since I had a proper bath. I started washing and then got my hair wet. About the time I got my hair ready to wash, I looked up and was surrounded by 10 or so

Marines. Josh, Seth, Cliff, Wainscott, Yeban, Hammett, Pena, Gio Garcia, Holloway and even the BN Chaplain was getting in the water. We all cleaned up, then just sat there and soaked and bullshitted. I was a brief moment of reprieve for all of us. It felt good to get clean and relax, if only for a brief moment. (There is a good pic of a bunch of us on one of our bath days) One the pics has myself, Jon Waters, Nat Reneke, Brian Murphy, Caesar, Cliff and Bobby Cox sitting in that canal soaking up the cool water. We all joked and laughed while sitting there in the water. A couple of the Marines, damn I can't remember your names, it's on the tip of my tongue. They were making home-made fishing poles, bobbers and gigs to try and catch fish, crabs and frogs from the canal. I heard they had a damn seafood buffet some nights. I absconded with about seven MRE beverage bags full of some of those rocks from that river canal. I made a fountain back home with those rocks and it was my little memorial to our fallen Marines. Back to the story. We finished up, and Josh's crew pushed back to Bulldog. I decided to stay with Seth and the boys, and had Josh relay that to Cohen. I got dressed and sat down to get the skinny on current TB TTP's around Helmond PB. I was told that they would take shots from the other side of the river, or from behind the PB in the thick corn and Marijuana fields. Same shit as everywhere else. I found me a spot to settle down and grabbed my coffee maker. I brewed up a batch and joined in a card game with the Marines not pulling gun duty. About hand number two, I heard shots being fired from the front corner of the PB. We jumped up and saw Seth behind his gun, scoping out for targets. Seth was a DM and had a scoped M16 for longer more accurate shooting. He called out he had sneaky fuckers at about 450 yards doing sneaky fucker shit. They were trying to lay in some IED's on a route used by Marines when they patrolled up and down the river area. Seth had em on the run and had already dropped one dude. Marines scrambled to get a line of sight on them and start calling out targets. I watched as Seth took a deep breath and began to squeeze slack out of the trigger. BAM! The round exploded out of the barrel and made its way to sneaky fucker number two. He had been on the run and hot footing it to cover. His mistake. The bullet traveled about 420 yards and hit the mark. The TB folded up like a wet rag and started his Virgin counting class in Paradise. I slapped Seth on the back and told him, "Great shot!" He didn't move and only gave me a slight head nod while he continued to look for more bad guys to give them another taste of Marine love. No more Haji's appeared, and we stayed up and on the lookout for a few more hours. I finally went back to my sleeping spot and stretched out. It was a good day seeing all the boys and getting some spa time in the canal. I fell asleep quickly and heard someone bitching about the freight train coming from under my poncho liner. I half assed rolled over fell back asleep. The next morning would prove to be just another happy day in Kablamistan for all involved. But this time we were giving it, instead of getting it. Get a beer and a snack! The party is still going. The Marines of 3/7 continue to win the hearts and minds of the enemy, by shooting them in the face or throat punching them on a daily basis.

CHAPTER 23

Cock Coffee.... mmmmmm good!

———

NOW EVERY MARINE UNIT I have ever been a part of, has always got a Marine running around half-assed naked. Whether it be back in the barracks or out in the field. Some guys just don't give a shit if their junk is hanging out or if their ass is showing. It is what it is, and more especially down range in a war zone. Field conditions are usually harsh and a regular bath and shave just aren't on the menu. You nasty bastards know who I'm talking about. Psssst.... Hey! Don't tell SGT MAJ Black that we didn't shave every day. He will probably try and come find me, so he can choke me out in my sleep. Oh, and I wore white socks some days when my issue ones were being dried, after they had been washed in the river. Keep that as our little secret in the LCPL pipeline ok? Ok! One Marine, LCPL Johnson, Kilo had two Johnson's and India had one, shit I can't remember his first name. Anyways, this Johnson would always run around naked with his hammer halfcocked, like it was no big deal. I called him "Beefy Tits" Johnson. He had the biggest man nipples I had ever seen. Not that I go around comparing man nipples, but damn son, cover those things up. The more you looked at them, the more you thought of ways to use them to your advantage. That's not being gay, that's just being a Marine in the field. I gave him shit, but he took it in stride and it was a running joke between us. He was a big ole boy and I think a machine gunner. All I know is I saw his cock more than mine during the deployment, but he was still a killer. Now Seth was pretty casual about his member as well and always wore his silkies like it was an order. I had settled in at Helmond and began my days with the old coffee and snuff routine. I had my SAT phone and always tried to make my calls early to get it done and begin my day. I let some of the

Marines call home, and it became a ritual whenever I broke out my phone, for everyone to get 3 minutes to call whoever they wanted. Thank you tax payers! It was an issued piece of gear and I never heard any shit from my civilian bosses about a phone bill. Anyways, I got a fire going for coffee and grabbed some standard issue tan paper cups. I sat on the back wall near the spa canal and made my call while the water got hot. I finished up and asked who wanted to use the phone. A Marine grabbed it and thanked me. I reminded him to keep it short and not let it turn into a jerk off session on the phone with Suzy call. He grinned and turned to make his call. I walked over to my coffee water, I was using a different pot, because my shit was still at Bulldog. I made sure it was the right temperature and began getting "Joe" ready to drink. Seth and a few Marines had gotten off watch and were sprawled out on their sleeping blankets they had acquired from the compound. It looked like a damn Harem bed chamber all piled together. Seth was in the middle wearing his silkies, all stretched out ready for sleep. I called out that the coffee was ready, and who wanted some? I filled a few cups and carried them to the Marines that were on watch. They grabbed them and thanked me, and I went back to the pot and filled some more cups. I then carried them over to where Seth and some Marines were laying down. I remember seeing Alex Kautzman, Emanuel Gonzalez, Giovanni Garcia and a few other guys laying around. About the time I got close enough to hand down the cups to them, Seth reached down into his silkies and pulled out that thing he called a penis, and shook it at me. He then said, "Hey old man, I got your coffee right here!" No Shit? I casually handed out two of the cups to the other Marines that were laying there. Seth kept shaking his cock at me and grinning. The Marines were snickering and grinning, waiting to see my response. After I had handed out the other two cups of coffee, I still had one hot steaming cup in my left hand. I knelt down close to Seth and reached out with my right hand and grabbed his cock like it was a snake trying to bite me. I didn't just grab it, I grabbed it and tried to pull it off his body. He screamed out and the Marines watching, started belly laughing and pointing at me, then Seth. I then inched up closer and put the hot cup of coffee right next to his junk. I looked him in the eye and dunked his cock into the coffee as far as that little thing would go. He howled and the Marines almost died laughing. You know that laugh where you stop breathing and tears come to your eyes. It was that kind of laugh. I let go of Seth and stood up over him. He grabbed his crotch and began cussing me in a steady Marine tirade. I kept looking at him and grinned. Then, while standing over him, I casually put that cup to my lips and drank the coffee in one gulp. I thought everyone was going to fall out with laughing pains. I finished the coffee and told Seth he could make his own damn coffee from now on. I think that is when LEP Actual became a true part of 3/7. That story has made its way throughout the BN, and I still get asked to tell it whenever I'm around some 3/7 boys. It's no bullshit and I really did it. Real world people scrunch up their face and think I'm a sicko or it's so gross. If you weren't there, then shut the hell up! It was just another moment in time while downrange, and I'm still not going to offer you any more damn coffee ever again Seth Rogers. The night passed with no attacks, and we began our daily routine the next morning. I was thankful to be close to the canal, and used it to clean up and cook whatever chow was on the menu for that day. Another Devil Dog from Texas, (are you seeing a pattern here?), Emanuel Gonzalez, took a group picture of all of us outside of PB Helmond. That picture can tell you so much if you just look at the details. All of you have my thanks for taking care of the "old man". I'm still planning my trip to South Texas to see Emanuel, to go fishing and eat some of those damn tacos he keeps teasing me with on FB. I helped on watch, then I talked Seth into letting me get behind the DM rifle for a while. Looking through the scope, I could get a much better look at details down range. I would scan the area, looking for Talibs sneaking around and doing what they do. By this point in time, the locals had started back with their daily activities, and tried to make it obvious that they weren't a threat to us. I kept scanning and looking, taking small breaks when my dominant eye would start to feel strained. Getting scope locked could take away your depth and detail perception. It happens when you focus too long on a specific spot and don't continue to scan. If you see something of interest, study it, scan around it then come back to it. You make a mental note of it, then come back and look for changes or an anomaly that doesn't fit what you are seeing. Our ROE was pretty open for any perceived hostile intent. If it was a developing situation, we usually called up PID and waited for approval. It if was an immediate threat, you reduced the threat with whatever weapons system you were on, and then called up your actions. If a bad guy was on a roof top looking at Marines through binos and had a radio, his ass was grass. Marines make the grass grow green, and were made to kill. If you saw a dude on a bike carrying some jugs, you might see him drop a jug on a pathway. Then another guy would show up and start digging in the area and act like he was tending to crops or fixing a spot on the path. After a while, shithead number three would come into the picture, and casually use his foot and push the jug into the hole and try to cover it up. After a while it was funny to watch. Who were they kidding? Their body language and turkey peeking from looking around was so damn obvious. The way they acted was a perfect example of the lessons I had taught Marines about Situational Awareness. I was watching and looking, when I got eyes on an obvious fucker digging in an IED. I saw him digging on his hands and knees about 300 yards from me toward the river between a canal and the river. Way down the river was a TB compound that became a trouble spot for us. Taliban would use it for a base of operations, and direct attacks from it. Marine patrols would take fire from there while searching the area. I saw him finish digging, then scoot over and grab a damn yellow jug. I yelled out to Seth what I was seeing. Seth came up and grabbed some binos and started looking. About the time sneaky fucker was bent over setting in the jug, I took a deep breath and starting wrapping my finger around the trigger. I asked Seth if he saw what I was seeing. He told me, "Fuck yeah, kill him!" The Talib was facing away from me and bent over the hole. His ass looked huge in the scope and I could clearly see his hands attaching a wiring harness to the jug. I was ounces away from the trigger snapping, when I saw pink mist coming from the bad guy's ass and head. Then the crack of a rifle followed. WTF? Apparently some other Marine had eyes on the same fucker I did, and was quicker on the trigger. From my vantage point, the round entered his ass and exited his head or chest. It was surreal to watch from the vantage point of the scoped rifle. Seth called up the hit, and Bulldog sent out a patrol to do a BDA and exploit the IED. I told Seth I was going to try and get some prints and evidence. Bulldog rogered up and sent the patrol to the spot. The Marines at PB Helmond would maintain an over watch position and cover the patrol. I grabbed my trash and loaded up to meet the guys on the way to where the bad guy fell. I started humping my way to link up with the patrol. They had a head start and where about 100 yards from the dead bad guy when they started taking SAF from the TB compound down the river area. Shit was flying everywhere and my fat ass was in the open with rounds zinging past me. I ran, well run is a loose terminology for me, I got to cover as fast as I could. I jumped down behind a small ditch that lead to the canal coming from the river, then got up on my gun. The patrol I was going to meet, had spread out and got a 240 into play. I saw a 203 popping grenades back toward the last area where we had taken fire from the TB. Little dust clouds were popping up every time I heard the 203 pop. I couldn't get eyes on the enemy and only saw Marines when I tried to focus in on the bad guys. I was dug in and the only way to take a shot was to stand up and expose myself. I was frustrated and pissed off. I really wanted to kill those fuckers shooting us. The enemy fire was shooting passed the Marines in front of me whizzing by me. I kept looking for a shot, but was scared to try and shoot past my brothers. I was scared to death, and feared a bad shot from me might be a green on green, or friendly fire tragedy. Damn it! All I could do was hold my ground and wait. It was only about 20 minutes of shooting, but seemed like a life time. My ass was hunkered down just listening to the firefight. Eventually the Marines were able to pull back and call for IDF or artillery support. I made my way back to PB Helmond by low crawling and duck walking to cover. I'm up, they see me, and I'm down. I must have looked like a retarded walrus on acid making my way back to Seth and the guys. They gave me shit and told me to get my ass inside the compound. I guess CPT Cohen had finally had enough, and got on the radio to get some IDF on the target. Marines had gotten into blood and guts firefights with the compound before, but the terrain was hell to push through, with visibility limited by the corn fields. Cohen got a HIMARS shot primed and ready to blast that compound to hell and back. We sat and watched the drama unfold before us. The Marine patrol pulled back and took cover to sit back and watch the shit show begin. I had a clear shot of the fun from the riverside corner of PB Helmond. The HIMARS shot shook the ground on impact, and rattled me to the bones. The after affects threw dirt and debris hundreds of feet in all directions. We knew it was a good strike, and any TB inside were hugging and kissing in Paradise. I mean they were always talking that "Martyrdom Bullshit". If that's what they wanted, then we were more than welcome to help em out. We sat and waited on a response, but none never came. It seemed like they had figured out that we weren't there to play games. We weren't fucking around when it came to killing the enemy. The effects of the hit were obvious, and we high fived and bumped fists. We resumed our daily grind and kept scanning for targets. The Talibs were probably at home licking their wounds, and didn't want to come out and play. Days passed and I returned to Bulldog to keep doing my LEP thing. Word from on high had reached us. GIROA had received complainants from the locals that we had killed 90 some odd innocent civilians taking cover in that building. That was such bullshit! The fucking TB had got their asses kicked and went crying to the locals. They had probably threatened them and made them spread the word that we had killed the "Innocent" people. I know that way up the chain, a discussion was had about doing a no shit BDA and TSE assessment to address the complainant. Hell it had been days since the strike, and anything remaining would be unrecognizable. I don't know if the BDA ever happened. I do know I was never told to go search for evidence at the spot, and I never saw one take place. We kept on patrolling and shooting. The sneaky fuckers kept on being sneaky, and we kept on shooting them in the face. I knew that our time was coming, I just didn't know when or where from. I continued to help with what I could and got into a daily rotation. CPT Cohen was always pushing out and looking to take the fight to the enemy. He never really had to look too hard to start a fight. But all I in know is, I can still hear him motivating and pushing Kilo Marines wherever he went. The Marines loved him, and he lead from the front. I can close my eyes and still see that huge ass dip of snuff hanging from his bottom lip, parading up and down in front of the Marines before the initial push. His words are still ringing in my ears, and have become a Kilo Co slogan. It may not be verbatim, but it is what I can recall. "No matter what you have done, where you have been, you are gonna get what you have been waiting for, what you are hungry for, and you will KILL THE ENEMY, KILL THE ENEMY, KILL THE ENEMY!" Fucking Ooh-Rah Sir! Take that hill Marines, breathe fire!

CHAPTER 24

Reach out and touch someone!!!

———

OPERATION "SMASH YOURSELF IN THE Balls with a Hammer" was still ongoing. I lost track of days and kept doing what I could, or what I thought I could do to help out. The different PB's kept taking sporadic fire or getting hit with SAF and RPG's on a daily basis. CPT Cohen would push out and check on his Marines at the different locations, and guide the LT's on tactics and plans of attack. Every time one PB would get hit and kill the enemy, the sneaky fuckers would back off and regroup, only to try and hit another PB or patrol. They never really overwhelmed us once we had dug in and had taken control of the area around the "Cohen Expressway." They were some hard headed bastards and kept on trying. I couldn't figure out where in the hell they kept getting replacements from. We had stacked em up like cord wood and kill a shitload of the TB. I made my way down to PB FIRES with Josh and his boys. They had been patrolling in CAAT trucks and supporting the dismounted Marines on patrol. We bullshitted and sat around while Cohen met up with a local Afghan elder and an ANP Commander. They talked and did the KLE thing while Marines scanned the area and held a security posture. We were in a tree line on the other side of FIRES and used the shade to keep out of the heat. Ryan engaged the local with his terp, and I heard him give the Afghan his usual approach. "My Marines our here to provide security for you and your people, you are either with us and the Afghan Police and Government, or you are either with them, the Taliban, you have to decide." Straight and to the point! As Always! He never was disrespectful to the locals, and he always tried to provide what medical or security assistance we could. But shit, I could see his point. We were doing the job they should have been doing. We will carry the load, but you have to help us help you. I got up and walked over to Ryan and tried to listen to the Afghan's response. He just nodded his head and then proceeded to ask for whatever he thought he could get from us. Usually money for a prized goat or sheep that we had killed or some family property we had blown up. It was usually just bullshit and had never happened. But if it had occurred, we tried to make it right with a payment offer. Most times the fact that the TB was using a family compound to attack us or shoot from was left out of the equation. The CPT finished up with the KLE and said his good byes to the local. He turned and saw me, and shook my hand. He then introduced me to the Afghan ANP Commander, and explained who I was and what I did. I gave the Commander the usual Afghan greeting and hug. We talked through the terp and just bantered back and forth for a little while. Cohen rallied up his guys and got ready to continue on to another PB, to keep spreading love and motivation. The Commander jumped in his truck and headed out. I told Ryan I was gonna hang at FIRES and see what was what. He made sure that I would check in with 1st SGT Woods, to keep track of my whereabouts and accountability. I assured him I would and proceeded to go inside Fires. I cleared the HESCO's and entered through the back entrance. The compound had a courtyard and several attached rooms and an additional building to the back facing out. Marines used this one as a sleeping area, the inner rooms had been taken over by LT Brent Birchum as a CP/TOC. I went inside the CP and had the radio operator call back to Bulldog that the LEP was at FIRES, and that I would check in as needed. I patted Birchum on the back and said hello. He was deep in the middle of a pile of maps and plotting locations with his grease pen and writing down notes. I didn't want to bother him, so I stepped out to see the rest of the boys. I went into the back sleeping area and hooked up with Martel. He was laying down watching some other Marines play cards and solving the world's problems. We shook hands and I sat down with the guys. We talked and caught up on what was going on. The Marines looked ragged, but they were still motivated. Typical Marine talk was heard. Bitching about wanting to go hunt and kill bad guys, Jody fucking Suzy back home, shitty food, rats, goats, bugs and dirt, blah, blah, blah. Now remember when I told you about the Peach orchards and the Hooch that was never made or drank by any known Marine or person that I knew. This is probably about the time that any of that didn't occur. I can neither, confirm or deny any of that kind of activity occurring at any place or time while deployed in the AO. If you do exist or have ever existed, you know who you are. Thanks Bro! It was a good batch! I mean theoretically it was a good batch, if it ever existed or had been drank. I kicked back and grabbed a dip of snuff and kept bullshitting with Ranson and the boys. Marines changed shift and pushed out to go on watch or whatever duty they had been assigned. Ranson was also a DM and had his rifle close and at the ready like all good Marines do. I told him about the chance I missed back at PB Helmond, on the IED fucker and about the HIMARS strike on the compound. He filled in the gaps about the activity at Fires and how the Taliban were still probing and taking shots at them. I listened and asked questions as they came to mind. The day turned to evening and the heat started to give way. I told Ranson that I was gonna catch a combat nap and get some zzzz's in before I attempted to cook some evening chow for the boys. They had a garden at their disposal, and I thought I could make a decent redneck dinner that would be different from the usual MRE or concoction they were making. I got some snores in and was starting to dream about getting shot at and bombs going off. I was dreaming and in my dream, I could hear RPG's screaming and Marines yelling to take cover. It seemed like mortars were dropping in and landing in my dream. Then I realized that it was real, and I could hear someone yelling, "Incoming, take cover!" Damn, again? This shit was getting old! I rolled over and couldn't find my vest or rifle. I had rolled over to the wrong side! I turned around to look for my gear and get my bearings. Rounds were striking the walls outside of where I was. The sun was setting and shadows obscured my view looking out toward the back of the compound. I quickly got my shit together and ran out to where the Marines were setting up to fight. Mortars splashed down within 20-25 yards away from the front of the where the Marines were waiting to engage and kill the bastards. I made my way to Ranson and asked if he saw any movement. He shook his head and kept looking for targets to engage. In my peripheral vision, I saw LT Birchum and a Marine with a radio, move up on my right side. The air was alive with rounds coming in and going out. I saw an RPG cutting through the air and fall short of the mark. Its initial line of approach was right on the path to hit some Marines that were off to the side and forward of where I was taking cover. I could see a Marine open up with a SAW and then the steady DMFD cyclic of a 240 started. Ranson fired off a shot and kept scanning for more sneaky fuckers to kill. I saw some Birds approaching the area behind the Taliban fighting positions. I started looking for movement and targets to engage. The Marines around me kept up a steady stream of lead toward the TB. I heard Ranson cut loose again, then a Marine call out, "He's down!" Enemy movement was covered by the corn and Marijuana fields, and only the impact of the bullets could be seen hitting around us. The HELO's engaged with their guns and the enemy fire suddenly stopped as quickly as it started. Marines stayed on their guns and kept looking for people to kill. They were amped up and itching to continue the fight. "Fuck you, you fuckers!"- could be heard from somewhere down the line. The gun run stopped the TB from shooting, and got them on the run. Behind the crop fields was an open area leading to a tree line. The bastards broke from cover and started running for the trees. Once in the open, Marines laid down a gauntlet of fire with their machine guns, and the Marine riflemen started taking precision shots at the remaining enemy. Ranson stayed steady and waited for another shot. The attack was basically over, and the Marines were giving back some lead to the remaining fuckers running for cover. I saw a group of four Talibs break through the corn and scatter toward the tree line. I took a shot and saw my target stumble but not go down. As continued to track him, I tried to steady my breathing for another shot. I adjusted my aim and placed the recital of my ACOG on the Talib's head this time. I aimed high hoping to get a torso shot. Squeezing the trigger, I let loose with two shots and saw my guy hit the dirt. No time for high fives, I pushed my sights to the right to engage the other insurgents. They had run farther than my guy after he had stumbled from my first shot. I didn't know how far they were, but I knew it would be a difficult shot for me. I scanned again and tried to keep up with their movement. They were dodging and ducking Marine fire all around them while doing the Afghan mile. I finally started to track on one fucker when Ranson dropped him like the sack of shit he was. It was a really good shot on the move, and proved that a Marine with his rifle is a force to be reckoned with. The few remaining bad guys packed their shit and high tailed home, or wherever they called home. We stayed up and in position till after dark. Making sure the TB didn't want to come back and try again. After the engagement, I went back into FIRES and met up with Birchum. Brent was a big ole boy and always had a great demeanor. He was also from Texas and we automatically got along well. He was smart and had taken the ball from CPT Cohen in regards to leading from the front and pulling his Marines by leading the way. We were bullshitting and hanging out, reliving the earlier fire fight. I kept noticing that Brent was scratching and rubbing his arms or his face. I didn't really take notice till he couldn't sit still while we were talking and continued to scratch. He was fidgeting and scratching himself like a Meth Monkey that had taken a bad hit. What the hell was wrong with him? I finally got a little closer to him and saw the reason. He was freaking covered in red welts and bug bites. That boy looked like he had his ass whooped by some Afghan Killer Chiggers! No wonder he was scratching like he was sitting in an ant pile. Damn son! I asked what the hell he got into. Brent told me he was out on a patrol and laid up to watch an area for enemy movement. By the time he had made it back to FIRES he was on FIRE! He looked like a damn leper. He shrugged it off as just another daily kick in the balls. I told him I was gonna stay at FIRES a few days to see if I could help out. He gave me a thumbs up and turned back to continue his work. I walked out to the open courtyard area, and met up with my Puerto Rican brother, SGT Pablo Colon. Pablo was another crazy fucking Marine that didn't give a shit about anything except his Marines and killing the Taliban. He was tough and direct, and didn't really care, as long as you did what you were told when and how he told you. Back in training before we deployed, he kinda blew off my TSE training at first when he had to pull Marines to go. Eventually I had got into his hip pocket and he came around. I know how he felt, he just wanted to kill TB and take care of his Marines. Roger that, I'm tracking! I'm proud to say we are still friends and talk regularly through the internet every week or so. Pablo is back home going to school to be a Doctor. A Doctor? Pablo is a killer. Who would have thought? I heard a story about a certain Puerto Rican SGT, that won't be named, that smoke checked a rabid donkey, and then he lit it on fire in order to deny the enemy access to said donkey. I don't know who that was, or if it ever happened. I can only imagine who that could have been. I know Pablo will achieve his goals because he never quits. I'm proud of him. Good job, bro!

I grabbed a spot to sit down and we smoked and joked for a while. Some of the boys shuffled through and grabbed some chow or cleaned their weapons. I remember Zac Dinsmore, Levi Unzeiteg, Hayden Patterson and a few others being there. They were good men and I could see that they were feeling the effects of being out in the field for so long. Uniforms were dirty and torn, their bodies had lost weight and their skin was sun burned and dark brown. But you couldn't see or hear any real complaints. Just the usual Marine bitching about everyday life. They pushed themselves every day, and continued to fight and kill. I just sat back and watched em continue their chores and talk among themselves. I caught myself thinking about the everyday citizen back home. They had no clue about the sacrifices made every day by these men and the other Marines I was with. Having a toilet, hot chow that they could choose from, a bed to sleep in, any of these things that were taken for granted every day back home. Oh yeah, don't forget not getting shot at or blown up by a crazy lunatic mob of Taliban, hell bent on taking the head of an Infidel. I was proud to be there to witness it in person. In reality, I don't know if I had any effect on the fight taking place around me. Probably not, but I tried to do my part. Hell, I was just another piece of the puzzle that the command had to track and be aware of. But I was never treated that way, and when I tried to step up, I was never told no. Unless it was an obvious risk out of my lane of expertise. I appreciate that and I know that came from the top. I hung out a few days at FIRES and never really got to get out with them on any face to face contact other than the firefight behind the PB. I group hugged the boys and jumped on a CAAT truck with Patsy to go back to Bulldog. I remember looking back and seeing FIRES getting smaller behind me. It was a sentimental moment, and I kept thinking about my boys. I was old enough to be their Daddy, well at least most of em. A combination of fatherly, brotherly and Marine pride welled up inside me. I must have gotten some of that damn Afghan dirt in my eyes, because I could feel a tear or two trying to spurt out. I turned around and waited on the next adventure that lay ahead. One of the Marines was playing some damn Disco music from an Ipod, and I heard em singing along to the music. I laughed to myself and was deep in thought of what I had done, where I had been, and the heroics I had witnessed up to this point. Little did I know, I had not seen shit yet? Blood and Sweat could be wiped away, but Fear was a constant fight to keep away, at least for me. I wasn't all, "Zombie mode, Oh I'm scared, help me!" Just that thought in the back of my mind. Always just on the cusp, never really spilling over. I was scared for the boys. Losing another Marine, was the fear that I fought.

CHAPTER 25

Bite 'em in the face!

I'M GOING TO START THIS chapter off with a tactical pause, and try to catch you up and fill in any gaps that have occurred. First off, I want to recognize CPT Chris "Mickey" Maloney, our KILO FAC. His easy going nature and steady approach was a blessing. A really good Marine and a fine officer, who has become a good friend. Still craving that Yuengling bro! While I have been telling my story, other than the Marines around me, I didn't know what else was going on in the Battalion. Whatever we heard was just scuttlebutt and made its way to us through the LCPL pipeline. Back in Musa Quala when we were on the hill, a pretty large IED was hit by a LOGCAP convoy that had brought out a re-supply. One of our supply Marines was Adam Harpold. Harpold weighed about a buck o five and stood as high as my chin. He was fun to be around and I used to have him show his "War Face". He would strike a pose and give me a scowl doing his best "Pvt. Joker" impression. Harpold got hit pretty hard by that IED as well as another Marine and Gunny Martinez. Nelson refused treatment, but Harpold and the other Marine were hurt and transported. Nelson just shook it off and stayed in the fight. Eventually his head trauma would catch up to him and I think Ahern had to order him to stand down and seek treatment. I remember unloading water and the blast occurring just yards away from me. I was shielded from the blast by a stack of frozen water bottles that had been unloaded from one of the trucks. I also remember that the first notion I had about writing this book was after Perry and his boys were in their bad ass gun fight down in the "J". I remember smoking and joking with the boys and I broke out my journal and read a few lines. Josh Matthews was there and started giving me shit about it.

His was always quick with a comeback and we always gave each other hell. I hope you're doing well brother, and now you can say I kept my promise. You are in the damn book. I know Josh and his crew were steady handing out love and happiness to the sneaky fuckers wherever they found em. I know we had several Marines that had single and double amputations to the legs. There are so many Marines with individual stories I can't write about because I wasn't there or heard their story. I am sorry about that, and it is a shame. Every Marine in 3/7 from that summer should have their own book as far as I'm concerned. Gunny Lucan Lacy became a great friend, and mentored me throughout the deployment and even back in 29 Palms. He and his wife would invite me over for dinner and treated me like part of the family. Master Guns Orlando Zuniga, with his brash hardnosed style, even kept me under his wing. He was a late arrival to the unit and just appeared out of the blue one day during training at Mojave Viper. He was another Texas boy from San Antonio, and just like the SGT MAJ, no one gave any shit to Master GUNS! On one of the convoys I had a full TSE kit get blown up and I lost a bunch of evidence and several thousand dollars' worth of gear. I had to make do with what I had or could find to use from my stash. One day MGUNS showed up carrying a huge backpack and then Orlando said, "Here fucker!" I looked at the bag and asked what it was. He told me to open it, so I did. I don't know how or where he got it, but it was a brand new TSE kit. It was even better than my old one, it was one of the new Blackhawk bags with shoulder straps, and it had newer and updated equipment. Just little shit like that along the way from the people in charge and from the Marines on the ground, made me feel a part of the team. All through my adventure of bouncing around the AO, I was always accepted and it was easy to fit in. The XO, MAJ Scott Conway, was another leader I was glad to have on my side. I know he was always up to his ass in paperwork, and a steady check list of things to do. But he still went out of his way to check on me and ask what I needed. And Sir, I know it was your effort that got me the commendation from the BC. I remember you asking about what I had done and my different engagements. Miraculously all that same info was in the citation I received. I thank you, I just want you and LTC Tipton to know that when I received that award, I was truly honored and appreciative. CPT Neilson, always moving around like a bull with nowhere to go. We gave each other steady shit. I know he and LTC Tipton were probably just waiting for me to drop. Knowing that I was out of my element and my nasty body was in no shape to play. Thank you both for hanging tough and letting me develop through your guidance and patience. I know that once I showed them I wouldn't quit. They could count on me to get it done. It wasn't easy, that's for sure. Every Marine that I came across during the deployment, had some part in helping me make it through, whether they knew it or not. Oh and thanks again Master GUNS for making me take that damn PT test before we deployed. I think you were trying to kill me before we even got started. Gunny Lafayette Waters was another Marine that was always there to help me and do whatever was needed. You couldn't high five or hug Waters, but he was a constant rock in whatever shithole we wound up in. He hooked me up with new uniforms after Musa Quala, and made sure I was good to go. Hope all is well and am glad you were on my side. LT Chris Parks also guided me and stepped up when called. An Auburn boy, I had to poke him with Alabama stories and keep him on the defensive. There are so many Marines that deserve my thanks and recognition. Most of these guys helped me for the past few months, tracking down pictures and timelines for my book. I can't thank you enough. Like, Ryan Rieman, Mouse, Ken Rick, Noel Gran, Andrew Ghabel, Jake Hunter and Nick Bellais. I remember hearing that Nick had started his own Afghan petting zoo, by catching and taming some damn hedge hogs back in Farah, during the first part of the deployment. These are just a few I want to thank. Also, Marines like Julian Billmair, Justin Sedelmaier, Darryl "Chuck" Charles, Rob Jones, Zane Kutch, Milan Franklin, Jake "Mouse" McMillin, Bryan Coughlin, Mafnas, Anis Abuzeid, Matt Almquist, Andrade, Bagby, Barrone, Batenhorst, Belcher, Billmair, Brasher, Campochiaro, Baby Ando, Debonis, Dexter, Dinsmore, Dobie, Ebbers, Epley, Escutia, Fann, Fettig, Fontanetta, Fraclose, Fraley, Frick, Jacob Fry, Fryxell, Garinger, Jimmy Goodwin, Groth, Haynie, Hulbard, David Ibarra, Infanti, Kehoe, Brad Jones, Kelso, Kinne, Kranzler, Kremer, Krikke, Linneman, Anthony McMahan, McPherson, Sgt. Moser, Lukas Myers, Nesbitt, Nguyen, Nikzad, Nowicki, Ocampo, Pete Opalacz, Ped, Pellegrino, Pinney, Zach Reiff, Mike Schroeder, Settlemire, Doc Testa, Doc Bisbee, Nat Small, Strobel, SSGT Suarez, Tamayo, Justin Swartzel, Trexler, Vucsko, Matt Walters, Brandt

Warman, Warvel, SGT Wiseman, Jesse Swayze(Yeah that Swayze!) and Vincent Yeban. These are just the Marines and Sailors that I can remember. There are so many more Marines and Sailors that deserve a heartfelt appreciation from people back home. I just want to recognize all of them. Not just the ones I've named, but more especially the ones I haven't. Oh, I can't leave out that crazy fucker Drew Crossland. You always have Marines that are good to go in the rear. Then you have the type that are let out of their cage in war. Most Marines can do both. Crossland was a killer and excelled in a fight, usually with a cigarette in his mouth, and a machine gun in his hands. Crossland killed a shitload of bad guys wherever he went, but he was a nasty, insubordinate fucker. But you could count on him to kill, then watch your back no matter what! Salty, old school Marine! You are a crazy bastard Crossland. Love you, no homo! (I'm glad you didn't throw you know who off the roof that morning, now take off that snivel gear!) Hang with me while I try to get back on track. I was back home at BULLDOG after my time at FIRES. I slipped back into my daily routine of coffee and chow, playing cards and just waiting to get shot at. The Afghan local that owned the compound we were in, made contact and wanted to speak with CPT Cohen. He had been coming around for a few days but nothing had been set in stone about any type of compensation. We set up a KLE and he showed up in the evening. The Afghan showed up and I went out with Ryan to listen to the conversation and try to use my "cop interrogation" skills to help out if I heard some hinky shit happening. The Afghan had brought another local with him, so we sat down outside the compound and began our Q and A. The owner was complaining about something and obviously saw us as the local bank. He was digging for gold and hoping to get a pay day from his perceived grievances. I kept watching his partner and saw that he was looking around at all the Marines and weapons systems. He was steady rolling his prayer beads in his left hand and counting. Not counting like a normal prayer count, but steady looking at Marines and counting beads. He then turned and looked at the different guns up on the wall and counted them off while touching his beads. The owner was still yammering to Ryan and I could see he was getting nowhere fast. This went on and on till finally a break was called and we got some water and stretched our legs. I told Ryan what I saw and I thought dude number two was a bad guy trying to recon us. The CPT told me to stay close and keep watching shithead when they started talking again. They settled back down and sure enough, shithead started looking at the MRAP's and counting them off with his prayer beads. I leaned over to Ryan and told him what was happening. Ryan quickly turned to shithead and said something through his terp. Apparently shithead understood what he said because he responded in English. English, well, well, well, what do we have here? It became clear that this fucker was a TB sympathizer and was scouting us. Ryan jumped up and called a quit to the KLE pronto. Words were exchanged, and they hot footed it out of the area, quick like. We huddled up and the CPT gave the Marines some instructions. I followed Ryan back inside and I heard something to the effect of, "That shit pisses me off, I want to bite em, Bite Em in the Face!" I don't know whatever happened to the owner or shithead. I never saw them again. The next day I got to get out on a patrol and try to get some TSE in for evidence. But really it was just to get the hell out of the PB and see what kinda of shit we could get into. We had a couple of ANA with us and started out toward FIRES. Half way across, we hooked to the right toward some local compounds. Locals were out working and in the fields. If they were out and about then we usually didn't have any contact with sneaky fuckers. It was when we didn't see anyone milling about. That was when the shit would hit the fan. We approached a qualat near a crop of corn and grain. A local fighting aged male was in the field working with a few younger boys. He saw us and approached. As he got close we had our terp tell him to stop, and turn away from us. He complied with a look of hatred on his face. A Marine walked up and patted him down for weapons. He was clear so we motioned him over to us. He immediately started talking to the one of the ANA soldiers that was with us. The terp told me that he was asking the soldier why he was with us and not fighting for the "Holy Warriors". I shook my head and told the terp to ask if I could talk to him. The local walked closer to me and let me ask my questions. I started off by asking who owned the field and if the TB helped them with their crops. Then I asked him if the TB took care of his family while he worked and provided food or water for them. He started looking at me like I was the Devil. I kept on! Then I asked how many kilos of poppy the TB taxed him and his family every year so they wouldn't get harassed or killed. I finally asked if he was a Muslim, and if the TB he was calling "Holy Warriors" were Muslim. He quickly responded yes. I then asked him if it was true that all Muslims were supposed to help other less fortunate Muslims if needed. Didn't Mohammad say so and that it was written in the Quran. He just stared at me for a moment then nodded his head yes to the terp. I then asked if he knew who Abraham was, and weren't we all sons of Abraham? (This is my Christian belief, and not what everyone believes!) He stood there in disbelief, scratching his head. I then dropped the bomb on him and asked him if he had read the Quran. He said no. I reached in my cargo pocket and pulled out an English version of the Quran. I showed it to him and told him I read it and I know what Mohammad said and that he even believed in Jesus (Esa) and in his mother Mary. They are mentioned more in the Quran than Allah and Mohammad. I then told him if he knew that Jesus was coming and everyone would have to answer. I left him there wondering who in the hell was that Infidel? I grinned to myself and kept on walking past him. Hey I'm a sinner every day, but I know where I came from and where I'm going. What is the old saying, know your enemy like he knows himself, and then you can answer his questions in his own words. It was a little mind trick that would keep him guessing for a while about who the hell I was. We patrolled out and never got into a fight or saw any bad guys. I made it back to Bulldog and found my spot to get some rest. Played some cards and bullshitted with the boys. The next day I was summoned to get my ass to FOB Nolay and hook up with WPNS. What the hell was happening now? India was working out of Nolay and I think CAAT Red was supporting them from there. The deployment was dragging on and I was starting to feel it. I kept having that felling of something big was going to happen in the near future. Little did I know that the something big was coming soon? Prepare to get your ass kicked. I thought I was ready. I hope you are.

CHAPTER 26

Nolay....a 1000 Taliban and a 1000 IED's!

———

BY THIS POINT IN THE deployment, I had gear and shit scattered all over Afghanistan. I guess I left stuff at Deleram, and in Bulldog, as well in some of the CAAT trucks I had been in. When I finally made it to Nolay, I found the CP/TOC tent that Calvin had set up to coordinate and plan from. He hugged me and asked how I was doing. It was good to see him, but he was in the middle of ten things at once as usual, so we didn't get to talk long. I dropped my gear outside the tent, then started checking out my surroundings. I heard a voice behind me say, "Who the fuck are you and what are you doing?" I spun around to see Ahern giving me a shit eating grin. I walked up and shook his hand. It was good to be back with WPNS. I felt at home and asked how everyone was doing. Steve walked me to the backside of the CP tent, to another smaller tent that was attached. He pointed to a cot in the corner, and told me that was my hooch. All my shit was neatly tucked under the cot and in typical Marine order. I saw some items I hadn't seen in months. Steve saw the question on my face, he told me he had collected and stored my gear for me. When India had pushed to Nolay, Bennett, Newsom, Josh, or someone had brought my extra trash with them to try and get it to me. I really appreciated it! I had clean socks, uniforms, and more TSE gear that I desperately needed. Carin and Steve took care of me, and had watched my stuff and made a spot for me when they got the word I was headed their way. Nelson Martinez popped in the tent, and we quickly shook hands and caught up on scuttlebutt like old friends. I noticed Nelson was a little hazy looking and slurred his words a little. I didn't say anything to him about it and let it ride. Nelson left to go whatever the hell Gunny's do, leaving me and Steve back at the tent. I asked

Steve about Nelson, and what was wrong. Gunny had refused treatment from his initial bomb blast back at CP Hill. He had been hit a few more times, not counting the one from the truck we were standing by when I got hit. He kept pushing himself till his head pain would make him drop. Typical hard headed Marine! Steve told me about the upcoming clearing op. WPNS would support India, while they pushed out to the village area and took control of a bridge and several compounds. The word was that the TB had re-enforced with 20-30 fighters. By this point in the fight, LT Newsom had been hit hard from a bomb blast and had to be transported out of the AO. SSGT Bennett took command of the platoon. The plan was to have INDIA 1st and 3rd PLT clear up to a bridge area and take control of that and several compounds. The Marines were to clear, hold and eliminate the bad guys. The op was set for a few days away. I got some rest on my new high speed cot. It had been so long that I since I had slept on anything but the ground, I didn't know how to act. I got some shut eye, and didn't wake up till Ahern starting yelling at me to shut the hell up from my snoring. I rolled over, gave him the finger, and then fell back asleep. The next day, I went into the CP and got caught up on any current info. I walked around Nolay looking for a shitter and place to clean up. I found the facilities and put them to good use. I meet up with Steve and he took me over to the Brit Marines side of the FOB. He introduced me to their SGT MAJ and some other Commandos that were there. After the meet and greet, we headed back to our tent. I had heard that India had lost a Marine a couple of weeks earlier while out in the area on patrol. Steve told me that LCPL John Newton had been struck by enemy fire when his patrol had been ambushed. Newton succumbed to his injuries, and was another Marine that gave his life to an unknowing nation. I never knew "RJ", but Verice told me he was good kid and a great Marine. Newton never gave any problems, and was always there to do what was expected of him. As a father I ached inside for the loss I knew his family was feeling. CPT Calvin finally hooked up with me and instructed to me stay close in case Marines on patrol, needed me to support them for TSE. I started staying in the TOC, monitoring the radio and waiting to get out to help. 3/7 INDIA had suffered some losses, especially equipment and vehicles. If I remember correctly, we had another Marine unit (2/4 I think?) supplement us by arriving in the NOLAY AO, and start patrolling in conjunction with our units. One of these Marine patrols got hit and called for CASEVAC. I remember Gunny Martinez hustling up a QRF to go help the downed Marine. Army SF was in the area and tried to help out with air support and over watch from above. It turned into a clusterfuck quickly, because all the different units were not on the same radio freqs. Gunny made it on scene, but the Marine had already been transported. That was a good thing, but Nelson and his crew got into a shit storm trying to get back to NOLAY. Calvin was hot, but eventually Nelson made it back and the hurt Marine was accounted for. The fog of war was present and waiting. We just didn't know how bad that fog would become. A few days passed and I was starting to pull my hair out from being cooped up like a dog on a chain. It was dusty as hell with "Moon Dust" all around. Every time the wind picked up, it was like a damn mini-sand storm. That shit would get everywhere. I could have been a "Millionaire", if I owned a baby wipe factory. We used them on our asses, weapons, faces, laptops, IPods, glasses, radios, ears, noses, wounds, feet, shit even on the dogs, you name it. If it had dust on it, the good old baby wipe was the answer. From the TOC to the vehicle staging area was a couple hundred yards. In between was a bunch of mud compounds, with a small alley way that was used to zero weapons. I asked Steve to get me some extra ammo so I could re-zero my rifle. He hooked me up with the rifle ammo, and threw in some extra 9mm for my pistol. I grabbed a MRE box and scribbled a target onto the box. I strolled to the range area and busted loose with some rounds. I had my rifle spot on and pocketed the left over 5.56 for my load out. I then walked up to 7-10 yards from the target and shot a magazine from my issued Beretta. My weapons checked out, so I headed to my hooch to clean em and chill out till evening chow. The day passed without any more drama. I remember getting a great night's sleep that night. The Brit SGTMAJ had allegedly given someone a green glass bottle of an unknown substance that magically appeared in my bag as a good bye and thanks gift. (I mean their bag) It hit the spot! I mean it would have, if it was something, I don't recall, Sir! The following day, the point element of Josh Waddell, SSGT Mark Juarez and their Marines, were out patrolling when they were hit hard by the TB. They were laying the ground work for the clearing OP to come. Probing the TB and gathering Intel by fire. They were taking fire, when one of the Marines was struck in the side SAPI plate. A direct ambush had been triggered by the TB and the India Marines were in the shit. Ahern told me to get my shit and stage at the ECP so I could push out if needed. I hustled up and grabbed my TSE kit. As I started for the ECP, Calvin yelled out to me. He said they had two fuckers in custody and I needed to process them for prints, then TQ them for HUMINT follow up. Hell yeah! That's my job, I was jacked to finally get back on task. I ran, jogged, and walked, as fast as my fat ass could go toward the pickup area. I made it to the spot, waiting for an INDIA truck to show up. I didn't know if I was going out with them, or if they were bringing the bad guys to me. On one side of the staging area was a small LZ surrounded by HESCO's on one side. I stood waiting, and motioned to the Marines at the ECP. I yelled out that a truck was in bound and to let em through as quickly as they could. The young Marines gave me a head nod, then a thumbs up. I looked at my watch and realized it was 9-11-10. Wow! That day from nine years ago was the reason for why we were all there, here and now. I stood there reflecting on all the events that had lead me to be standing where I was. It was kinda surreal. I wasn't even a small part of the solution or fight for freedom. I knew that! Shit, looking at the big picture, I was like another speck of sand on the beach. But I was proud of who I was with, and proud to be helping the Marines do their part of the fighting. I snapped out of my day dream long enough to see a MRAP hauling ass through the ECP without stopping. It was headed toward me, so I started walking toward it. As the truck got closer, I could see a Marine up in the turret yelling at me and waving his arms. I had been at the staging area and had no radio with me, so I didn't know if my status had changed. The truck got up beside me, but kept on going. What the fuck? As the truck passed, I could hear the Marine yelling my name saying, "Ronnie, hurry, come quickly!" They stopped next to the LZ, so I ran the 30 or so yards to get to them. As I approached, the back driver's side door flung open and I saw SSGT Juarez almost fall out of the arms of a Marine. Mark had a massive head wound and was bleeding profusely. He was unconscious, and I knew he was in a bad way. I grabbed him around his shoulders and eased him to the ground. All the Marines in the truck piled out and ran around to help. I had one of them grab his feet, then we carried him clear of the truck, toward a spot near a HESCO. I told one Marine to go to the TOC to advise them about Mark. I had another find a Corpsman. I did a quick body scan with my hands, then grabbed a dressing from my IFAK. Mark already had a dressing on the wound, but it was hanging loosely from his head with blood seeping from it. I re-wrapped it, then added my bandage on top. The Marine returned from the TOC and told me a bird was on its way to get Mark. I then took the middle knuckle of my right hand a pushed it into Mark's sternum. I got a slight response when he opened his eyes. He couldn't talk, but he reached up with one hand to push my hand away. That was a good sign. He felt pain and could react. The Doc showed up and we got him ready to transport. Minutes later, the bird arrived, and I helped carry him onboard. The word I got, was that Mark and his Marines had been ambushed by the TB. It is unknown if the Marines were lead out of place or if the Taliban got the jump on them. Juarez had moved up to check on the Marine that had been hit in one of his side SAPI plates. Mark was trying to cover their movement to counter ambush and kill the fuckers before they hurt or kill more Marines. When he leaned up to throw a smoke grenade, he was hit in the head by a Taliban sniper. I hope that sumbitch is ass raping all the goats in Paradise that he wants. I got to see Mark several months later in Austin, Texas, where he was recouping at a special brain trauma treatment center. He really didn't remember much or me at the time. Since then he has been retired from the Marine Corps, and has made a remarkable recovery. We talk by txt every once in a while. OOH-RAH Brother! I never did get to hook up those TB detainees. I went back to my hooch and cleaned the blood off my hands, wishing I had some more of the juice from the green bottle that never existed. Two days later, my boy, Verice Bennett, would earn his place beside other Marine Warriors that are talked about with honor and pride by Marines from past and future conflicts around the world. India had stayed out in the thick of it, with Josh and Verice maneuvering their men across the battlefield. 13 Sept 2010, the day of the planned clearing operation for INDIA. They pushed out knowing that the enemy had strengthened themselves with 20-30 shitheads. Verice and Josh knew the route was full of IED's. What they didn't know, was the TB had a little more than 130-150 fighters, with hundreds of IED's spread-out in the path leading to the objective. The Marines numbered about 60! A thick layer of fog rolled in the area. That caused CAS to go red, which meant air support was a no-go. Verice and Josh, along with their Marines, had pushed out under the cover of darkness early that morning, getting eyes on the objectives. They improvised and dug in to harden their fighting positions as best they could. As the sun began to crest, it was a signal for the TB to step their attack. Under constant fire, with a barrage of RPG's and mortars, 1st and 3rd PLT pushed to the bridge, holding their ground. Then the PLT's pushed to each of their target locations while under steady fire. Dodging fire and a steady path of IED's, elements of 3rd PLT took cover in a compound only 30 meters away from an enemy strong hold. The Marines were in a constant fight against mortars, rockets, machine gun fire and Taliban snipers. INDIA 1&3 were in a shit storm and it was stacking up all around them. Marines were shooting and killing the sneaky fuckers in bunches. Every time the Marines would stop an assault coming from one direction, they would receive SAF from another. The TB where hell bent on 'Jihad', and wanted some Infidel blood. Bennett called in several HIMARS, with one danger close at the enemy compound 30 meters away. Every time Verice would cut loose with a strike, Josh would have to call for his own support element of IDF. At one point, Verice grabbed some grenades from one of his Marines, throwing and striking some Taliban fuckers trying to close in on their position. I heard that he did this several times. The Marines were surrounded, with ammo running low, when fix bayonets was called for. After almost ten to twelve hours of fighting, and several HIMARS strikes, the Marines had stood tall with Verice leading his men with his calm cool manner. Josh was leading and fighting with his killers at the same time. During the course of the battle, the enemy had closed to within 10 meters of the Marines. I was told that the real numbers were hard to believe if you weren't there to witness it yourself. Verice and Josh had called in so many rocket strikes, that Leatherneck had run out of rounds to shoot. The Marines were cutting loose with 10's of Javelins, 155 Excaliburs, 11 HIMARS, and an ass-load of 120mm mortars from NOLAY. At one point they were dropping their own internal mortars up and down on enemy targets at 40-50 meters within their perimeter. No Shit! I know Verice or Josh don't consider their actions that day as Heroic. I know that the Marines with them, showed their own individual fighting spirit as well. Just like they had before and continued to do. But SSGT Bennett's action that day earned him the Silver Star. Eventually he would also be awarded the GySgt John Basilone award for Courage and Commitment. Love you brother! Semper Fi! Also to the Marines that stood side by side him on that day, you have my appreciation. Every one of you should be individually recognized for your Courage and Commitment. No words are needed to express my feelings for these men. Men like Josh and Verice and all the other Marines from 3/7, are the type of men that make our Marine Corps the finest fighting force in the world. I am so very proud of you all. Break.... Break....ah....Blade Actual to LEP ....over..... LEP here.....go ahead Sir.....get your ass to Jackson...... Roger that Sir....LEP en route ......over and ......out!

CHAPTER 27

And the, "I don't give a Fuck Award goes to...INDIA CO!"

FROM MY PERSPECTIVE, IT APPEARED that INDIA got the short end of the stick. I guess my 'Man Crush' on Josh Waddell was still in effect. I missed him and his guys, and worried about them. My buddy, LCPL Luis Maldonado was somewhere in the mix with INDIA. I'm sure he was doing his thing, toughing it out like the rest of them. They were constantly tasked with setting up blocking positions to support their sister companies. But just because they didn't get the "Glory Runs", don't think they weren't kicking ass and taking names. They had faced the sneaky fuckers wherever they went. Then, the INDIA Marines killed them wherever they went. The LCPL pipeline was full of scuttlebutt in regards to what INDIA was dealing with. They were in constant motion, and the big fight I just wrote about in the previous chapter, was only one of a handful of heroic actions that they participated in. INDIA was always in and out of the wadi, either north or south of the Sangin Green Zone. One lovely shithead vacation spot, was referred to as the "Green Mile". It was a section of the wadi, that was covered with the Jungle all around. Farm crops, stacked with corn, grain, vegetables, and of course Marijuana. All of these were interconnected by irrigation canals and local compounds. Of course the sneaky fucker hiding places were scattered in between. On one such occasion, they had set up on a cliff area near a river bank, in order to get a better advantage point from high ground. The Marines had been taking harassing machine gun fire from across the wadi all afternoon. But what the bastards didn't know, was that Gunner Carpenter happened to be tracking INDIA's movements. Shame on em! He magically appeared the way he always did! Gunner

Carpenter and his crew rolled in to assist the Marines. Josh and the boys were steadily taking sporadic machine gun fire from across the wadi, from some shithead wanting to have a duel. They would get some RPK or PKM fire, then once in a while a single round from a heavy gun would blast around them. I heard that Gunner, Josh and the rest of Marines dug through rock, and concrete like shale, to emplace their heavy weapons. They fucking toughed it out and continued to dig with their hands and e-tools to set up the weapons. Throughout the night, they continued to take SAF, but never quit fighting or working to get their weapons ready. Stop and think about that. The BN Gunner, the PLT CO, were right there, side by side their Marines, doing the work that needed to be done. That is leadership by example. Not do what I say, but do what I say, then do what I do! If they didn't get it finished, they would be wide open to enemy fire without their weapon systems ready to fire back. Make it or break it baby! They made it. But if you know Gunner or Josh, was there really ever any doubt? When the sun came up, they were in a position to take control of the AO. The advantage of being dug in with a 50 cal., a TOW, and a MK19, was the key to them being in control. Beside the fact of pure motivation by nasty, killer Marines. They could lay down a massive amount of fire now. Gunner had the TOW Marine get it up and on possible targets. The Marine on the TOW was scanning looking for the enemy fucker shooting at them with a heavy machine gun. Gunner had been paying attention to the timing and impacts of the incoming fire. He turned to Josh and said, "Those bastards are firing a DUSHKA one round at a time, like a sniper rifle!" At first I'm sure, he thought that Gunner was bullshitting him, or had been in too many IED blasts. What? No way! Well maybe? Once Gunner said it, then explained it, it made sense. No shit! The TOW gunner had just finished scanning the area, then took head face away from the optic, when "BAM!" A single 12.7mm projectile from the DUSHKA, exploded on target, by hitting the optic of the TOW, causing it to shatter. The Marine behind the optic was cut from glass and debris. But lucky and alive! Fuck! What now? They had a TOW but no optic. Well, leave it to Gunner. He did the magic Gunner dance, and a new optic appeared. I'm sure that if they had needed a timing chain and a bearing for a 52 John Deer PTO drive, Gunner would have made one appear or fall from the sky. They were able to put the

TOW back into play and blast the shit out of the machine gun fuckers across the wadi. This was just one of many unknown fights that INDIA had to endure. They never quit, and kept moving and fighting as directed. Eventually they pushed into the southern green zone and another big fight ensued as told earlier. Josh and his boys had to self-recover their own vehicles at times when they went down, with no support. Suck it up Marine! What else could they do? They sucked it up and pushed forward! 1ˢᵗ PLT got down to nine Marines after KIA/WIA's had reduced their numbers. No truck? Fuck it start humping! So they did! Then I heard about LCPL Luke Stansted. This killer had figured out the TTP's of the TB sniper team that was giving them hell. He broke it down to Josh, and was allowed to lead a four-man element, to set up a counter ambush on the sneaky fuckers. After hours of sitting in the dark, Luke and his Marines not only found the Taliban sniper moving with his spotters. But they executed a text book ambush of the bastards. They smoke checked the enemy sniper team, and left em to rot. These are just a few examples of how INDIA continued to fight and support the big picture for the Battalion. The INDIA Marines had gone to one of the only small PB's held by the Brit Marine Commandos. The Commandos had given them shit about where they were headed, and told the INDIA Marines they would never make it. The Brits wanted to fight, but were limited on support from their superiors in the rear and at home. After watching how the US Marines performed, they were impressed. I'm fixing to piss Waddell of with this story. I heard it from someone who was there and witnessed it go down. I trust them, so he can get pissed. This is what I was told. After the Brit Marines had witnessed INDIA kick ass and take the fight to the Taliban, they were impressed. After the fight, the INDIA Marines made it back to the Brit PB. Josh had a head shed with the Brits, and met up with their Senior NCO. After the brief, the conversation turned to typical Marine banter. Then Josh asked to trade an American shoulder patch he had, with the Commando's Senior NCO, for one of their Brit unit patches. The British Royal Marine Commando was so disgusted by the lack of British determination to fight, that he tore off his Royal Marine patch and gave it to Josh. "Take it Sir, it doesn't mean shit to me anymore!" The Commandos are some hard bastards and can stand next to anyone in a fight. That shows the determination and grit that the INDIA Marines displayed on a daily basis. If that doesn't make you want to throat punch somebody, then you are either not a Marine, or you are a Pussy! I also heard the tales of SGT Will Tresseder. He was a former GRUNT that left active duty, then transitioned to the Marine reserves to continue college. He was getting a Master's Degree from Stanford! Freaking Stanford? When the surge happened, he volunteered for the first Marine unit headed downrange. He was attached to INDIA as a CAG rep, or Civil Affairs Group. Apparently he was still a grunt, because he would stand toe to toe with the other Marines in whatever fight they got into. After he returned home, Will finished his degree. Congrats Brother! Then there was Killer Delarosa. LCPL Joe Delarosa 0311, the forever point man. I heard that he could sniff out ambushes and IED's like a hound on a pack of coons. His attention to detail, and killer instinct I'm sure saved a lot of Marines. Then the time INDIA performed a local MEDCAP with their DOC's. MEDCAP's are great tools to gather Intel on the local bad guys, as well as get the atmospherics of the locals. A local Afghan father brought his small malnourished daughter to be treated from a head wound. The little girl was about three years old. She had taken a piece of metal shrapnel to the head from an IED blast. Fucking Taliban! Anyways, the father was told that she needed surgery before the metal continued on to her brain and killed her. The Pashtun father sat and thought about what the terp had relayed to him from the Doc. He casually replied, "She will die, I will not have another man touch her or violate her." What the hell? How do you help people like that? The Afghan turned and walked away with his daughter. Then there is the tale about Doc Anthony Leveque. All Navy Corpsman care for their Marines. That is a storied tradition, and their heroics are never forgotten by the men they save. While patrolling in trucks along the "Green Mile", Doc's truck hit, resulting in a Marine being seriously wounded. Without regard to his own safety, Doc Leveque rushed to the hurt Marine under fire. Doc engaged the enemy with his weapon, attended to the hurt Marine, called in a 9Line for a CASEVAC, all while staying the fight to help his brothers. Just another unknown act of bravery that has gone untold. I'm going to go back a little bit to when INDIA was still up in the Golestan area from the first month of the deployment. This is a crazy-ass story and needs to be heard. It's funny as shit! The Marines were on the FOB or PB. Shit I can't remember. But anyways, a couple of young looking local Afghans came up looking for help from the Marines. One of the guys was is a bad way and was looking like he was about to drop. The Marines were letting them inside, when about that time, the sick one passed out. Grabbing a terp, the other Afghan told them that his buddy had been bitten by a Cobra. (The snake, not the HELO) They got the sick Afghan inside the aid station to try and help him out. The Marines called for a bird to transport him to get the antidote and attention he needed. But as usual, the birds were busy and unavailable. The Doc tried to make the kid comfortable, and was sure he was going to die within a few hours. Nothing could be done! The friend was upset and beside himself. The Marines tried to console him, but it was a struggle to get him to calm down. An hour passed, then another and another. The snake bite Afghan was still alive! The Doc was re-checking the sick Afghan when he noticed some weird injection looking marks on his body. His vital signs were slow but steady. He was fucking high as a kite on heroin when the snake had bit him. The dope slowed his metabolism down so much that the venom just cycled through his system without killing him. Wow! Only in Afghanistan! You had to be there to believe it! These are just a few of the types of things INDIA had to deal with on a daily basis. Semper Fi you nasty bastards! Did you really think I would forget about you? No way bro! Carry on…..LEP….out!

CHAPTER 28

Jackson....and the Royal Marine Commandos!

―――

NOW IF YOU KNOW ANYTHING about British soldiers, you know they are some hard mother fuckers. They want to find and kill the bad guys just like us. The only problem was their government didn't really support them. Any death of a British soldier was just too much for England to handle. It was what it was! Look at all their special units, SAS, SBS, Marine Commandos, Air Regiment, and the list is ongoing. Shit we stole what they had perfected, and turned it into the basis of our own special ops units at different levels. Gotta respect that. I had made my way to FOB Jackson in the heart of Taliban country. It was one of the most dangerous places in the world at that time, and still is. The Brits were still there, and we co-habitated with them until they went home. I always got along with them since my time in Lash Kar Gah back in 2007. They are smart asses, direct and full of themselves, so we got along great. I came in on a convoy through the heat and dusty wadi route we had taken. I remember seeing a burnt out Blackhawk or Pavehawk helicopter as we pulled into Jackson. It was the remnants of an Air Force PJ rescue crew that had been shot down trying to fly some wounded out of Jackson. It had been shot down just as it cleared the HESCO's. It fell just outside the FOB, and was drug back inside. It was a reminder that we were still in the shit. Jackson had a river canal running behind it with a bridge connected to Afghan counter parts and other elements and buildings. I climbed out of my truck and dropped my shit. Looking around, I could see Big Jessie and Francisco from Lima. Then I saw Kilcullen walking to the front of his truck. I ran over and set up an ambush on the other side of the truck and waited. As soon as Jullian cleared the front of the bumper, I bear hugged him from behind and squeezed.

He kicked and flopped but I didn't let go. It was good to see him and his guys. It seemed like it had been forever, instead of just 2 months. We chatted and bullshitted for a minute or two. They had to attend to business, and I needed to find a hooch before dark so I told them goodbye. I drug my bags toward the TOC to check in and see what the deal was. I could see the BN guidon flapping in the breeze, so started walking toward it. I left my gear outside and popped into the tent. I saw CPT Nielson, and Gunny Lacy. Derek was head down as usual, working on something. Lucan waved at me and motioned me over to him. He asked how I was, and if I was good. I filled him in on the high lights and asked him the same. As we were talking, Derek walked up behind me and slapped the shit out of me on the shoulder. That was how he kissed. I spun around and we jokingly squared off. I really wasn't gonna fight his big ass, I might shoot him, but not fight him, too damn old, I'm brittle. We shook hands, and I really think that I had finally earned some respect from him for hanging tough, sticking it out. He said things were crazy with trying to RIP the Brits, then RIP with 3/5. On top of the daily operations and daily bullshit that the sneaky fuckers kept throwing our way. I made it quick and pushed out of the TOC so he could keep working. Lucan followed me out and helped me carry my stuff to a HESCO hut that was used for our sleeping quarters. It was HESCO's all the way around with a dirt floor covered in plastic walking pallets, and a hardened roof. It was a really good bunker/barracks place to sleep. I was moving up in the world. I got my gear settled, then Gunny gave me a tour of the compound, pointing out the different places I needed to know. The chow hall was an outdoor open tent area that you kinda rotated through so everyone got a chance. You hurried up and ate and got the hell out. We were walking around so I could get the lay down, when I ran into Master Guns. He gave me his typical, what the hell are you doing here look, and asked if I was going to do anything except eat chow and sleep. I told him I planned on sleeping, but I would get up and eat when he came and got me throughout the day. He told me to fuck off or some other romantic words, and walked off. I grinned and kept looking around. I found a spot behind the chow area that we used to hang out and play cards in the evening time, when-ever Marines weren't on patrol or on duty. After evening chow, I headed to the TOC for the daily BUB. I had nothing to offer, so I sat and listened. After the

BUB, the OP's O pulled me off to the side and gave me a quick low down. I was in Fobbit mode and was to stand by in case I was needed for any TSE. Check in daily at the TOC and always have someone know where I was. Roger that, Sir! FML! So, I basically hung out and waited for something to happen. I started staging up toward the back gate behind the LZ. I had some shade and could see out of the back of Jackson pretty well. Second day at Jackson, I see patrols going out on foot. Lima heads out toward the river, away from Jackson, and the Brits would head toward town. Sometimes our Marines would do a joint patrol with the Brits and hit certain locations in town. The HUMINT, PSYOPS, GOV Affairs, or specialized units like that would go out to meet their local counterparts. I sat there and watched patrols come and go throughout the second day. After lunch time I heard some shooting and the FOB come to life with activity. British Royal Marine Commandos were running around grabbing ammo and mortars and Javelins. I thought it was cool that they could wear shorts and t-shirts. Shit, LTC Tipton would rip one of your balls off and shave you himself with a butter knife if he caught one of us dressed down like that on duty. I sat and watched, as the shit show started around me. BAM! Fucking mortars started landing all in the LZ, they were walking up toward me. I heard some snipers open up above me. The Brits had that bad-ass .338 Lapua with them. Get some bitches! I saw some Brit Marines scramble up, about twenty feet away and set up a mortar. They started cutting loose with rounds. The incoming increased, and the wall directly behind me started taking more and more rounds. The concrete cracked and splintered. This went on all day for hours till evening chow. It was a bit disturbing, but I didn't realize that we were in the Heart of the Shadow Government for the Taliban. We were on the outskirts of Sangin city. Sangin was their strong hold, and we were only 100 yards away from the main road going to the Sangin market. I went to bed and got up the next day, and the same shit happened again. Then the next day and the next. Fuck me. I was going ape shit crazy just sitting there. Finally, after a week of this bullshit harassment, it got real, real fast. I had bullshitted with some of the British Marines and started waving and saying hello to the ones I recognized. We shared a couple of fags and had some tea after evening chow. I guess I had watched 5-6 days of this shit. Patrols going out, and then getting shot at all the way back inside the

FOB. Behind Jackson toward town was a big open field thick with vegetation and grass, then a canal, and finally city streets leading into town. On day five or six, I was in my hiding spot staying out of the way. I had opened up my knife sharpening business and was making 20-25 cigs a day from the Brits and 3/7 Marines. So I'm dipping snuff, rubbing a knife on a stone, and I see a patrol headed out. I waved to the boys and asked how long they would be gone. Typical Brit smart assed answer was given. But it turned out to mean a couple of hours or so. Those boys couldn't understand my redneck speak, and I had hell with their accent as well. They pushed out and I sharpened knives. After a little while, bullets started popping and hitting around me and all throughout the FOB. Fucking mortars started landing, then RPG's came splashing in. It was the real deal! I ran to my hooch and geared up. I grabbed my rifle and headed back toward my spot by the back gun tower. By the time I made it back, we had both US and British Marines on the wall shooting out. The gun towers were shooting almost straight down and at the HESCO walls. Some Brit Commandos rallied up under the gun tower and were planning a hasty QRF. They had their ATV with a wagon ready to load the wounded. I got closer, as more fire started coming directly in the FOB near the gun tower. One Brit, turkey peeked the corner and cut loose with 2-3 bursts of his rifle. They carried a bullpup designed 5.56. The weapon was reliable and functioned, but the mags they were issued were shit. I had brought a double PMAG with extended round capacity, so I didn't have to reload for a while on the first engagement. One Commando's rifle jammed! As he worked to clear it, I stepped up to help. The Commando relayed to me what was happening. He said that the patrol had been hit and were fighting for their lives. They had been ambushed on the way back in and the Taliban fuckers were actually stalking them, shooting at them as they tried to make it to the FOB. Two Marine Commandos were down in the field and bleeding out. The buggy would push out to the edge of the field, then load the wounded, while the foot patrol and QRF would cover by shooting and bounding its way back to the FOB. Shit, son that's not good! He cleared his weapon, and re-engaged, fucking jam again! He pulled back behind cover, so I then popped out, got on a bad guy and laid down some shots while he cleared his weapon again. I saw the Brit Marines running for their lives, and fucking TB busting through the grass 10 yards behind them shooting wildly. I put some rounds into a black manjam, then went back to cover. The Brit took over and started outside the FOB to help cover by fire. Second round out, another fucking jam! The Brit Marine was cussing and trying to clear his weapons a third time. I reached up and yanked his rifle out of his hands and handed him my rifle with the 60 round magazine. It still had 57 or so rounds left in the double stacked magazines. He started popping targets and walking toward his men. I followed behind and dropped the piece of shit metal stamped magazine from his rifle, and threw in a 30 round tan PMAG from my vest. Fuck it, let's go! We buddy drilled and covered each other all the way to where they picked up the wounded. The bullpup shot like a greased pig with the PMAG, I had no problems with it. It took a second to get used to the standing PIN reticle, but I got good results. We made our way to his other QRF guys and took up a position on their left side. The patrol that had been hit, was behind us and were getting the wounded back inside. They threw a couple of grenades and killed two more Taliban trying to run back to cover. One of the Commandos tapped me on the shoulder, then they tapped each other. I saw they were bounding by fire back to the gun tower on the corner of Jackson. I fell in and tried to keep up as best as I could. After we got back inside, the Brit Commando handed me my rifle and told me, "Thanks Mate, let's have a Fag!" We burned one really quick, then they were ready to move to go check on their buddies. I handed him his rifle, and told him I was glad I could help. He started to drop the PMAG that was in his rifle to hand it back to me. I told him to keep it. It was obvious that he needed it more than me. He told me thanks and slapped my shoulder. I don't know how, but Steve heard about my little engagement and he gave me shit about it. Something to the effect of, why don't I go to England, then I could join their Marines if I wanted to just run around outside the FOB shooting all Wild West style. Kiss my ass! Anyone of you would have done the same. The TB got pushed back and went back to whatever shithole they called home for the evening. The next day I pushed out to the PGOV's house/office with Major Conway. The Boss had tasked me with starting an ISTK, an Interim Security Transition Kandak, or something to that effect. (Not sure on the name, so many damn acronyms I can't keep up!) Take locals, give em basic training and supplement them with the police like neighborhood watch with

AK's and glow belts. The provincial governor had to sign off on it and get the local leaders to recruit men for the job. The XO introduced me, then went to his meeting. I walked in to meet the Gov and his staff. He looked like and an old grandpa and reminded me of my granddaddy. He had them same stature and mild mannered way. He had me sit with him and we waited for some of the local elders to come in and get seated. He explained through the terp that he had a NDS agent that would vet the locals and coordinate their interactions with the police. The NDS agent arrived and I got up and walked over to him. To everyone's surprise, we hugged and held hands all the way back to my seat at the table. The agent was a friend, and we had worked together in Lash Kar Gah from one of my previous deployments. This was gonna be easy. The Gov was happy, and the local elders saw a way to try and get some more money, so they were happy. After the hug and kisses, I headed out and grabbed the XO from his meeting. He said he had more to do, so I headed back to my hooch. When I got there, I found a new 40 Commando Unit patch, along with a set of Brit tan uniform combat shirt and shorts, with a new British mess kit. I was surprised! Thanks Mate! I appreciate it! I stowed my new stuff before some Marine put his dick skinners on it and it disappeared on me. A few days passed with 3/5 Marines showing up to start left seat right seat transitions. I know I saw Big Jessie and Martinez, coaching and talking to their counter parts from 3/5. I heard that the 3/5 boys were motivated to be there, but the command had their own ideas of how to approach the Sangin problem. 3/5 Dark Horse would eventually have 25 Marines KIA. It is a tragedy to lose any Marine in combat. I feel for the families and pray for them, I hope you will to. What really hurts me, is when you look up SanginUSMC online, all you mostly see is 3/5 references. 3/7 was there doing the push before 3/5. We laid the ground work for them. 3/7 got face to face with the fuckers, and killed a lot of shitheads, way before 3/5 got there. Not taking away from 3/5, they did their duty and carried on, but we were there first. That is a fact, and 3/7 has earned the respect it deserves to have. Brothers of the Blade! Rah! The next day I was back at my knife sharpening business, when I heard a rocket go off on the FOB. Shit, Incoming? No second strikes were heard, and no gun fire. Weird! I got up and walked toward the TOC. Between the TOC, from where I was coming from, was a staging area covered with a camo net. Marines coming and going off patrol, would drop their gear there, then set up a gear/weapons watch or detail. Marines would go grab chow or whatever, and then return to their stuff. I guess the two Marines on weapons watch was bored as fuck! One Marine saw a M72 LAW rocket (I think it was a LAW, it was some damn type of man portable shoulder launched rocket!) and wanted to know how it worked. The other Marine was apparently proficient in how to use it, so he started calling out the numbers by order, on how to deploy and fire the rocket. The inquisitive Marine that had picked up the rocket, started to go through the functions of deploying the rocket, while the other Marine was laying down on his back. He had his cover over his eyes, while he continued to call out the steps in order. When he called "squeeze the trigger", the other Marine did, and that rocket shot out, straight up, through the cammie netting. It burned a hole in the plastic pallet floor from the back blast. This kinda shit put SGT MAJOR's into orbit. Black was quick to snatch up the Marines in question and start pulling out their fingernails while choking them, or whatever it is SGTMAJ's do to junior Marines that piss them off. The XO had me complete a detailed investigation and type up a report for the Boss. I never saw those Marines again, Hmmmmm? No telling what happened to them. Probably still being hazed to death by SGTMAJ Black. The Sangin city area was full of Taliban, and a living shithole full of IED's and ambush points. Marines would perform joint patrols with the Brits. Especially specialized Marine attachments that had to go out and meet n greet their counterparts downrange. A few days later, a Marine EOD attachment, MSGT Daniel Fedder would be killed by an IED while returning with a Brit patrol just a few hundred yards from the back gate entrance of Jackson. The area was so laden with IED's, the Brit Commander refused to push out any additional men, for fear of getting them killed by another IED and/or ambush. I heard through scuttlebutt, that the Boss, LTC Tipton, had to be physically pulled out of the Brit TOC, away from the Brit CO, before he choke slammed someone or just took over FOB Jackson by sheer will of force. If you know the Boss, you knew he could do it! You knew he cared for his men, just as much as he was a hard tough man. Even though Danny Fedder was an attachment to 3/7, he was still a UNITED STATES MARINE, by God! Before we went home, I helped Gunny Lacy gather and pack all of MSGT Fedder's gear to send home.

Danny's loss was a hard pill to swallow, just like the others. It was late September. We had a large combined memorial service with the Brits. I was honored to be in the formation during the service. I lost myself in thought, thinking of all the men that had given the ultimate sacrifice. We prayed together, then reached down inside ourselves, to grab the strength to keep pushing forward. I remember we were all counting days till we caught the freedom bird. I had finished up all my real duties, had the local Afghan security team thing going, and all my reports and evidence were pushed out. Shit, I kicked back and kept getting rich from my knife shop. I was the snuff and cigarette 'King"! That evening, I saw CAAT White roll in and start staging in the back parking area of Jackson. Cool, I assumed they were coming in to get ready to RIP with 3/5 to go home. Fucking wrong! I walked up and we all grouped hugged. Patsy and his guys told me to get my shit, we would be pushing out for a final clearing op within the week. What? Bullshit, I got 13 and a wake up, or close to it! FML....OK! I asked where? They pointed out the back gate, to the spot where the fields meet the city's edge, lined with shops and shitheads................

Sangin Bizarre!.......... Fuck me! <u>3/7 NO SHIT! NO SHIT 3/7!</u>

CHAPTER 29

The Final Push!

I DON'T KNOW IF LTC Tipton just wanted to give the Taliban a final punch in the face, or just keep doing what Marines do till the last minute. I was told we would push out and clear a large urban portion of the city, around the bizarre area. We had about 3-4 days till the time would come to go. Over the course of the past few months, there was a heavy concentration of sniper activity in and around FOB Jackson, as well as patrol areas in Sangin. I know the Brits had lost several men, and I believe we lost a Marine Engineer attachment, SSGT Bock to sniper fire as well. I even heard that the civilian tech that worked on the "God's Eye", had been hit. The "God's Eye" was a type of surveillance platform. Gunner had set up a "Hunt the Sniper TF", and I fell in, to help out with the task of tracking this fucker or fuckers down. We watched video and made a link analysis chart of all the POO/POI, with dates, times, and possible locations. Myself, Gunner, and Sgt. Lukas Vuscsko rotated around the clock, waiting and watching on the cameras, for the sniper to move or make a mistake. Gunner put all his knowledge and experience into trying to track that sniper or snipers. I heard that both Brit and U.S. Special Forces were also tracking these fuckers with their own surveillance and sniper teams. Additional intel showed it was probably foreign trained snipers, based on their TTP's. My guess would be Chechens. Some are Muslim that answer the "Jihad" call. Chechens are some hard 'sonsabitches', and have that "Mother Russia" training and background. Gunner finally narrowed down some key positions that matched up to the evidence he had put together. I know he was aching to get a shot at the bastard or bastards. I wasn't there when the shot was taken, but I heard that they killed one with a hellfire or JDAM a couple days after I had pushed out. Blowing one of his shoulders off at the arm. I never confirmed if Gunner took the shot, or if it was the SOCOM guys. After I was cut loose from "sniper watch", I hooked up with Patsy. He gave me the when and where to be for the clearing op. I went and changed into my silkies, then headed over to the canal to get a swim and a bath. It was so nice to cool off and just forget where you were. But that moment was usually cut short by the sneaky fuckers, with SAF or IDF flying around. Kiss my ass! You can't take a shit in peace, can't go swimming in peace, can't rub one out in peace, and you couldn't even sleep in peace most of the time. Early the next morning, I grabbed my backpack and trudged over to the CAAT trucks. Patsy found me a spot on one of his trucks, so I loaded my gear, then jumped on, ready to get it done. It was somewhere around September 27th, if I remember correctly. It was the day MSGT Fedder was killed. We wound up on a rooftop of a small police station or close to one. We had set up a TOW along with a 240 and other weapons, ready for when the time was right to kill these fuckers, then go home. We had an over watch position, with pretty good line if sight on the lay out of the area. It was still smoldering hot. So, we made some homemade shade out of sand bags and cammie netting. On one corner of the roof was a sandbagged fighting position with a makeshift roof. Patsy used that spot for his TOC area. I remember plopping down in front of him to take a picture. He was behind me, with his legs wrapped around me. I thought I might have felt a little "Chub" as he pushed his crotch up against me. Big Blakey was there, along with Patsy and the rest of the boys. I think Josh and the rest of the CAAT section was still down in the "J" by INKERMAN, in the area of the PB's, playing with KILO. Some Shadow guys creeped around the area, getting eyes on known shithead locations. A couple of the snipers popped up and began plotting some known locations on their diagram sketches and dope books. I bullshitted with Wainscott while he was up there checking out spots. They got the info they needed, then pushed out to hand out lead mementos to whatever bad guys happened to stumble into their crosshairs. I was miserable just sitting there. Fucking dusty and hot. A couple of Army PSYOPS guys were attached to us. They played their infidel messages on loud speakers throughout the day. I know it had to piss off the locals and Taliban. Because that loud shit was getting on my last nerves. We scanned and plotted enemy movement whenever we saw obvious bad guys moving in and out of the area. The afternoon came on, and the TB put their big boy pants on to come out to play. It started out with some sporadic SAF. It didn't appear they were on target, just spraying and praying. The volume of fire increased, then RPG's starting flying around toward Marine positions. We started spotting targets, then Patsy got on the horn calling them out. The Marines punished them and the dismounts closed the distance to the sneaky fucker locations. Rocket and rifle fire started concentrating on specific Taliban that were running in and around the compounds. The TB thought they still had free reign to come and go as they pleased. They had never had a unit close with them and get in their face to kill em before. The Marines were as crazy, as the Taliban were fanatical. I'm sure the bad guys had some 'oh shit moments' right before a Marine bullet punched a hole in the back of their heads. I recall SGTMAJ and the BC coming up to the roof to get an update and spread some motivation. Troy checked on me, then told me to hang tough because the push was on for the next day. I saw LTC Tipton coaching Patsy, giving him some instructions. After the quick head shed, they continued on to the other Marine positions they wanted to visit in the area. This cycle of back and forth fighting went on throughout the evening. It got dark, and it seemed the fight slowed down at the same pace as the sun going down. Once it was dark, we set up security a watch. I wasn't given a shift, but I would get up and relieve guys on watch as much as I could. They were in the fight, and needed the rest more than me. The push started in the early morning hours. It would continue on through 29 SEP 10. The next 48 hours, would be a moment in my life that I carry with me every day. Elements of LIMA were still out fighting on the river in order to cut off any TB that tried to maneuver back into the city. I think Big Jessie was leading his guys on the river. Francisco was back at Jackson with a guard force, and LIMA 1st PLT was set to go out as the QRF. INDIA 1st PLT had moved into the area. They set up an ambush patrol south of Sangin, to block any shitheads from moving into the bizarre area that tried to reinforce the Taliban that were getting crushed by the other Marines in the bizarre. LCPL Ralph Fabbri was a Combat Cameraman who was attached to 3/7. He wanted to get downrange to do his job, like all good Marines do. He linked up with the LIMA guys that were tasked with the ambush patrol. About the time that they had set up, the shit was hitting the fan in the Sangin bizarre. LIMA 1st PLT was set up around a tree line with a pomegranate orchard nearby. They had a small open area surrounded by trees, orchards and local Afghan qualats. I don't know who triggered the ambush, but I do know that Ralph was hit by a TB sniper round. It struck him between the main plates of his vest, and travelled bilaterally across his body. It was a terrible wound. He was young and strong, and his body continued to fight to live. I was told that Doc Koening made it to him under fire. When he got there, several other Marines were rendering aid to Ralph. Due to the fighting spread out in the Sangin AO, numerous casualties were being tracked by CASEVAC birds. It took over an hour for a bird to recover Ralph. During that time, the LIMA boys stood their ground protecting him, while fighting for their own lives. Doc Koening continued to use his skills to keep Ralph alive every time he slipped in and out of death's grip. They got him on a liter and pushed over to a compound to take cover. Bobby Burns had pushed out with his guys to help reinforce LIMA 1st PLT. Bobby said that Ralph was in and out of it. Bobby held Ralph's hand while Doc kept working on him. The whole time trying to revive Ralph, Marines stood fast while continuing to fight and kill the enemy. While in the fight to survive, one Marine had the box magazine of his 249 SAW blown off by a shithead bullet. Another Marine engaged that fucker and put him in the dirt. It was an up close, in your face firefight. Finally, a Brit CH46 made it on scene. I have been told that they performed a near perfect "controlled crash" in the small open field that was used as an LZ. They landed under fire, with the rotor blades of the bird just feet away from the tops of the trees. Marines scrambled while fighting and shooting, to get Ralph on the chopper. It was said the he was still fighting to live as they got him onboard. But the Good Lord had other plans for Ralph. He called him home, and just like that, he was gone. Semper Fi Brother! I know that LIMA kept fighting, and punched through the remaining TB strong points by the next day. Punch a Marine in the face and he will get up to finish the job. Way to hang tough boys! CPT McKinley, was pretty shook up, I was told that he took Ralph's death pretty hard. Just like all good Marine leaders, he cared for his men. Doc Koening, thank you for your efforts. LIMA 1st PLT, you define the essence of Marine Warriors! To the Brit air crew, thank you for helping your brothers when the shit was flying in your face. While all this fighting was happening, I was still on my rooftop watching the devastation that a Marine fighting unit can hand out to whoever pisses them off. We were killing shitheads as they ran for cover, or turkey peeked around corners trying to shoot at us. Marines on the ground were blowing holes through compound walls where the Taliban were trying to hide. Instead of going around obstacles, the Marines would use "DEMO" to blow their way through an object, then kill whatever fuckers were left inside. The enemy that would try and run, would get picked off by Shadow and other Marines. They really had nowhere to go. If they hid out in a compound, they would get blown out and shot. If they ran, they could get smoked in the open. Shame on em! The Taliban were fucked! I remember we were getting steady RPG fire from a TB hideout about 175 yards away. They would spray us with machine gun fire, then pop of a couple of RPG's at us. After the third or fourth RPG shot, we took a direct RPG round on the lip of the wall on our rooftop. A Marine called out he had PID on the RPG shithead location. Patsy told him to take him out with the TOW. We cleared the back blast area behind the TOW, while the Marine got on target. I was on the left side of the TOW, about three feet away when the round was cut loose from the tube. Damn…..Baby Jesus! It fucking streaked out across the surrounding rooftops toward the TB RPG location. I clearly remember seeing a Talib stick his head around the corner of the compound as the round was racing toward them. He had a AK in his right hand, and was looking in our direction. About two seconds later the wire guided missile impacted with a thunderous explosion. I saw the AK fly up and back, away from the sneaky fucker. I could also see a large portion of manjam that looked like it still had a man in it, start tumbling skyward. You fucked with the wrong Marines son! Get busy counting sheep! Once the dust settled from the TOW shot, that area was quiet of Taliban activity. I could still hear Shadow engaging targets in the distance. About this time, was when the radio traffic picked up with the 9LINE for Ralph Fabbri. We had Marine casualties scattered across the battlefield, but they continued to fight and kill the enemy. I can remember the fight progressing into a lull. Every once in a while you would hear a small firefight, then a boom. Marines would push forward and sweep the location. They continued to kill whoever they found with a weapon. It lasted till 29 or 30 Sep. Hell maybe even till 1 or 2 Oct. All I know is that we kicked the shit out of the Taliban. After the first 48 hours of steady ass whooping, the pussies couldn't handle anymore Marine hugs and kisses. The following days were a sweep and clear of the area. I wound up back up at Jackson with Gunny Lacy. I helped him with MSGT Fedder's gear. We sanitized it, then prepared his personal items to be sent home to his family. I was an emotional mess by this point. The light was shining bright at the end of the tunnel. But it seemed the tunnel was getting longer each day, instead of getting shorter. I finished any outstanding paperwork I had left remaining. Washed all my gear and clothes. Then cleaned my weapons. I put on a uniform I had kept stashed from 29 Palms. I kept my 'salty cover' on. The uniform was clean and brand new. It was falling off of me. I had lost about 50 pounds! I packed my bags, and just lived hour to hour on Jackson, out of the top of one bag. I was just waiting for my freedom bird to Leatherneck. A few days went by and I was getting anxious as a junkie looking for a fix. I can't remember the exact day, but before evening chow, MGUNS Zuniga told me to come to the TOC. I dropped what I was doing, then headed to see what the hell kinda shit sandwich I was being served now. I scrunched down through the tent flaps, then stood up in the TOC. It was a skeleton crew, none of the bosses were there. I asked where the honchos were at. A young Marine on duty pointed behind me, toward the adjoining tent that was used as a working office for all the different shops in the BN. I walked out and entered the office tent. LTC Tipton, SGTMAJ Black, CPT Neilson, MGUNS Zuniga, Gunny Lacy, MAJ Conway and the whole staff were present. I was thinking, "Oh Shit....what now?" MGUNS pointed for me to post up in front of the Boss. I was really shitting my pants then. As I walked up to face the Boss, CPT Neilson gave me one of his love taps to my shoulder and grinned. OK...maybe I was gonna survive! I stood in front of LTC Tipton, then saw SGTMAJ Black grab a red citation folder, with a certificate inside of it. I got in the best position of attention my old body would allow and waited. SGTMAJ Black read off an appreciation certificate from LTC Tipton, then handed the certificate to the Boss. LTC Tipton shook my hand and told me that he appreciated me, I had performed beyond what was expected of me, and he was proud of me. His words were like a sledgehammer hitting me in the chest. I felt a well of pride surging in my chest. He then handed me the certificate while slapping my shoulder. I know it sounds corny, but I had never felt such accomplishment since boot camp. All the staff shook my hand and congratulated me. I had to be quick and get out of the tent. Some of that damn Afghan dust had gotten into my eyes again. I stepped out to clear my thoughts and get a dip of snuff. MGUNS came out and grinned at me with that, "Hey Fucker" look he has. He then told me to have my shit ready, and be at the LZ at 1900, I was headed out. No Shit? Roger that MGUNS! We shook hands again, then I went to get my stuff ready to go. I remember that it was like being in a dream. I staged my gear, then kinda wandered around reminiscing about all the shit I had seen and been a part of these last seven months. The time came, so I snatched up my bags to get in line for the bird. I suddenly felt an overwhelming sense of fear. I shuffled into the chopper, then struggled in the dark, as I got buckled into my seat. I can still see the bird taking off and clearing the HESCO walls as it got airborne. I was free baby! Well almost. The sneaky fuckers had a good bye gift for me and the other Marines onboard. Hundreds of tracer rounds started dancing all around the HELO as it gained altitude. Fuck me! Just my luck. Make it all through the shit, then get pegged on the good bye flight. As luck would have it, we weren't hit. I looked down at Jackson, then the city lights flickering in and around Sangin. I raised my right hand and lifted my middle finger, as the tracers whizzed by the chopper. Good bye Bitches! Better luck next time!

CHAPTER 30

They are all Heroes to me

———

I MADE IT TO LEATHERNECK without any crazy shit along the way. We all hustled off the birds towards a couple of busses lined up close by. The buses carried us to a couple of huge GP 100 man tents in the middle of nowhere. It was at least a mile to the chow hall and PX. I guess the command at Leatherneck was scared to have "Killer Marines" wandering around the base looking for shit to start. We all settled in to a spot in the tents, then stowed our trash. We spent the next few days out processing as the other Marines from the BN trickled in by companies. After a week or so, we were ready to get stateside. We made it home on a commercial flight, back to where we started from. The ass grabbing and Jackassery was in steady supply. Who could blame them? The Marines deserved to be cut loose. We convoyed back to 29 Palms by buses. As we hit a long stretch of road leading to the base, you could see the Marine base pushed up against the mountains. It was an unreal moment, seeing the final leg of a journey that had stretched the globe and back. Once we hit our BN area, the Marines got into formation for instructions. The formation was quick and to the point, "Thank God!" There was a large "Welcome Home" contingent of wives, girlfriends, and other family members just waiting to get their hands on their Marines. It was a really good moment to see and share in. After a quick group hug, the boys spread out to find their people. The real welcome home party would have to wait a little longer. We had to stow gear and weapons. We all headed to the armory to secure our weapons and various killing instruments. It felt weird to hand my rifle and pistol over. I had been carrying a gun since I was 18 from my time in the Corps, then 20 some odd years as a cop. But during the past seven months, I did not go anywhere without my weapons. As I out processed throughout the BN, I was feeling melancholy. (I know that's a big word for most of you, just look it up Nasty!) I made a final tour of the BN offices and said goodbye. The boys had gone to their respective barracks or homes with their families and friends. SGTMAJ Black stopped me before I walked out. He squared up in front of me and shook my hand. He told me I was a part of the BN, and he expected to see me in Vegas for the Marine Corps Ball in a couple of weeks or so. I was thankful and told him to count on me. I got home and tried to settle back in with police work and normal life. As you all know, that's not easy after experiencing what we had. I made it to the Ball and back. Had a really good time with all the boys. Then over the course of the next several months, I was invited back to 3/7 for the Boss' change of command ceremony, and memorial for our fallen Marines. I was pleasantly surprised when I showed up for the ceremony. 1st Sgt Ahern was now SGTMAJ Ahern, as well as Big Daddy Krause. We met and bullshitted. Then Steve told me to go change for the ceremony. I looked puzzled, and told him I was ready. He told me to get my uniform on. He went to his vehicle and pulled out a set of Cammie's and told me to hurry. I was just lucky enough to have a pair of boots that would match. But I did pull a Gunner move, no T-shirt! I put the new uniform and cover on then saw that my name and DOD tapes were correct. (Thanks again Steve!) The ceremony began and I sat up front with Steve behind LTC Tipton. After the main portion of the ceremony was finished, Steve grabbed me and pushed me toward the Boss. We shook hands, and he then presented me with a Commendation for my actions while deployed with 3/7. It was a "No Shit" Commendation that I am so proud to have received. The commendation and the certificate from Jackson, is included in the forward of this book for you to read if you want to do so. I was invited to the O club to have a meet n greet with the outgoing and incoming 3/7 staff. LTC Tipton was presented the BN Guidon that had flown in Afghanistan wherever he went throughout the AO. It was encased in glass with a nice frame. Really cool! As the gathering continued, LTC Tipton called me over to the new BC and introduced me. It felt good to be recognized. I think it was at that moment I realized that all the shit and hard approach tactics by the Boss was for a reason. At the time we may have bitched, but we had done our duty, we had faced the enemy and killed them where we found them. The Marine Corps could be proud of the MARINES of 3/7. Over the course of the next few months I would again be assigned as a LEP to another Marine BN. I went back to 29 Palms as a guest of Cliff to watch him be awarded his Navy Cross. My step-son Andy, (I raised him, he belongs to me!) who was a fresh-ass boot Marine right out of Boot Camp, attended the ceremony. I had Gunny Martinez snatch and kidnap him from Pendleton. He got fucked with a little. But Nelson let him off the hook by telling him that he had been sent to find him by me. He got to meet a lot of the 3/7 boys and the Assistant Sec. of the Navy. Mr. Secretary coined him as he walked through the crowd after the ceremony. It was pretty special, and I am glad he got to see what real Marine Brotherhood is all about. I started this book as a field journal while downrange. I began by reading daily blurbs to the Marines at night. It has grown into a memoir of things I saw and experienced. There are so many people that need to be recognized for the courage and bravery they showed in Afghanistan that deployment. I have tried to portray the things I saw in the best way possible. But expressing the horrors of war can be difficult to write, as well as to read. The death of the bad guys doesn't really bother me at all. I have been dealing with bad guy death all my years as a cop. If they hadn't done what they did, they would still have 'Man Love Thursday' to look forward to. They wanted and tried to kill us as bad as we did them. They got "Lucky" (For them lucky, not us!) a few times. We were good a lot! But the memories of the Marines we lost, still lingers. My memory has been blurred by time and things I have experienced these past few years. I hope I have done justice to each and every one of you. Throughout the story you keep hearing me repeat my love for the Marines around me. It isn't being in love like a wife or girlfriend. It a love for a brother or child that you would kill or die for. I know in my heart that any of the Marines from 3/7 would die or kill for me. They proved that. I just want them to know I feel the same way. I have been blessed to maintain and grow friendships with hundreds of these men and their families. The bond is still strong and continues to grow. We have lost several Marines to different tragedies since we came home from that summer. As well as some on their next deployment to Afghanistan. Their sacrifice and commitment is not forgotten or diminished with their passing. I want to apologize to any of you that has felt slighted by anything I have said or told in my story. Some circumstances may be out of order or missing some key details or people. I am truly sorry and take the blame. I tried to get it on paper as I remember it happening. There were over 1300 of you, but there was only one True LEP! If I could list every Marine or Sailor by name and deed, I would do it in a heartbeat. If you don't see your name, then the fault is mine. Each and every one of you have my deepest appreciation for your bravery and dedication to duty, in the face of the enemy on a daily basis, in that place known as Afghanistan. Our nation owes you all a sense of gratitude that can never repay your Honor, Courage and Commitment. I'm sure each of you has that friend or family member that always wants to know about the blood and guts. Then when you tell em, they don't understand. Or they give you some excuse or reason why it was wrong or want to hold hands while kissing to help the bad people understand. There are people like us, then people that want to be us. If you aren't one of us, you will never truly understand. Lieutenant Colonel Clay Tipton Sir, I want to personally thank you again for not giving up on me, and letting me prove my worth. I hope I was not a disappointment, and you can still count on me to get it done. To Sergeant Major Troy Black, I appreciate your steady resolve and want you to know that your help was a big part in the completion of this book. Every brother Marine from 3/7 that sent me pictures and stories on FB and email has earned my appreciation as well. Thank you again, I have returned to the killing fields of Afghanistan several times since being away from 3/7. Doing different contract jobs for the United States government. Nothing has filled the void of my time spent with the 3rd Battalion 7th Marines. I guess I'm still looking for the bond of brotherhood I felt back then. But what can compare to the Brotherhood of the Blade? It has been six years since we all left together. I have struggled personally and professionally, with highs and lows. But I always reach out to my brothers from 3/7 to get me through. When I break it down, whatever I feel is nothing compared to the shit we all went through together back then. I did what I could to help when I could. I just want the world to know your story. If I don't sell one book, but everyone one of you that wants a copy gets one, then I will feel blessed. It is what it is! I don't know how to keep rambling on about my feelings and sense of pride I have every time I think of the Marines I was blessed to be surrounded by. The saying is true,

"Once a Marine, always a Marine!" You have proven that to me, and I am thankful. This is your story, not mine. I know it is told from my vantage point, and I hope it doesn't sound like, "Look at me, look what I did!" Any accolades or accomplishments I received are because of each and every one of you.

Semper Fidelis, God Bless you, and long live our beloved United States Marine Corps!

CHAPTER 31

Fallen Angels

———

THE FOLLOWING CHAPTER LISTS THE Marines that were taken from us too soon in their lives. I want to take the time to personally thank each of the family members of all the Marines that sacrificed everything they had for so many. I truly feel that their deaths were not in vain. They each answered a higher calling to serve their country. They were where they wanted to be, and doing their duty. Each of them stood tall with their fellow Marines, doing more than what was expected of them. I share with the family's pain and loss. I will never know the depth of your individual feelings. But, I can tell you that they were each loved by me and the other Marines as brothers. The strength and commitment they showed, while facing danger, is a testament to who they were and their fortitude. Each death was felt by the Command and the men that were beside them on those tragic days. I thank you again for giving them to us, and hope you will allow me to continue to pray for them as you do.

Sincerely, Ronnie Alexander, 3/7 LEP/USMC 2010

LCPL MICHAEL C. BAILEY USMC
3RD BN 7TH MARINES
KIA 16 JUN 2010
FROM PARK HILLS, MISSOURI. DIED WHILE SUPPORTING
COMBAT OPERATIONS IN HELMOND PROVINCE,
AFGHANISTAN IN SUPPORT OF OPERATION ENDURING
FREEDOM.

CPL KEVIN A. CUETO USMC
3RD BN 7TH MARINES
KIA 22 JUNE 2010
FROM SAN JOSE, CALIFORNIA. DIED WHILE SUPPORTING
COMBAT OPERATIONS IN HELMOND PROVINCE,
AFGHANISTAN IN SUPPORT OF OPERATION ENDURING
FREEDOM.

CPL CLAUDIO PATINO IV USMC
3RD BN 7TH MARINES
KIA 22 JUNE 2010
FROM YORBA LINDA, CALIFORNIA. DIED WHILE SUPPORTING
COMBAT OPERATIONS IN HELMOND PROVINCE,
AFGHANISTAN IN SUPPORT OF OPERATION ENDURING
FREEDOM.

LCPL ROBERT J. NEWTON USMC
3RD BN 7TH MARINES
KIA 23 AUG 2010
FROM CREVE COUER, ILLINOIS. DIED WHILE SUPPORTING
COMBAT OPERATIONS IN HELMOND PROVINCE,
AFGHANISTAN IN SUPPORT OF OPERATION ENDURING
FREEDOM.

SSGT MICHAEL A. BOCK USMC
3RD COMBAT ENGINEER BN
KIA 13 AUG 2010
FROM LEESBURG, FLORIDA. DIED WHILE SUPPORTING
COMBAT OPERATIONS IN HELMOND PROVINCE,
AFGHANISTAN IN SUPPORT OF OPERATION ENDURING
FREEDOM.

CPL CHRISTOPHER J. BOYD USMC
2ND BN 4TH MARINES
KIA 19 AUG 2010
FROM PALATINE, ILLINOIS. DIED WHILE SUPPORTING
COMBAT OPERATIONS IN HELMOND PROVINCE,
AFGHANISTAN IN SUPPORT OF OPERATION ENDURING
FREEDOM.

MSGT DANIEL L. FEDDER USMC
EOD 7TH ENGINEER SUPPORT BN
KIA 27 AUG 2010
FROM PINE CITY, MINNESOTA. DIED WHILE SUPPORTING
COMBAT OPERATIONS IN HELMOND PROVINCE,
AFGHANISTAN IN SUPPORT OF OPERATION ENDURING
FREEDOM.

LCPL RALPH J. FABBRI USMC
COMBAT CAMERAMAN DIVISION PAO
KIA 28 SEP 2010
FROM GALLITZIN, PENNSYLVANIA. DIED WHILE SUPPORTING
COMBAT OPERATIONS IN HELMOND PROVINCE,
AFGHANISTAN IN SUPPORT OF OPERATION ENDURING
FREEDOM.

GLOSSARY OF TERMS

107's- Communist Bloc type rocket (they suck!)

50 CAL- A U.S. Military large ass machine gun mounted, vehicle/tripod

9LINE- Template or system to call in support for fire or medical rescue

A10- U.S. Bad-ass Jet Plane with a machine cannon that kills shitheads

ACOG- Weapon optic or Advanced Combat Optical Gunsight

AGL- Automatic Grenade launcher, (they suck too!)

AK- Russian Bloc assault rifle (The main weapon of your enemy)

AMMO- Ammunition

ANA- Afghan National Army

ANAL- Ammonium Nitrate and Aluminum explosive

ANFO- Ammonium Nitrate and Fuel Oil

ANP- Afghan National Police

AO- Area of Operation

Apache- U.S. Military type of attack helicopter

APOBS- Anti-personal obstacle breaching system, explosives man portable

BAF- Bagram Air Field, Afghanistan

BC- Battalion Commander

BDA- Battle or Bomb damage assessment

Bird- Helicopter

BN- Abbreviation for Battalion

B.O.- Body odor, which I had

Bobber- cork or floatation device used for fishing

BUB- A Daily Battle Update Brief

Blackhawk- Military type helicopter

C4- Military grade plastic explosive

CAAT- Combined Anti-Armor Team

Cache- A stash or holding area for contraband or weapons

CAS- Close Air Support

CASEVAC- Term for Casualty Evacuation

Chi-Com- Chinese communist type

Chocolate Starfish- That place where the sun doesn't shine and poop comes out

CID- Criminal Investigation Division

CP- Command Post

CPL- Abbreviation for Corporal

CPT- Abbreviation for Captain

COBRA- U.S. Military type of attack helicopter

COIN- Counter Insurgency term

COL- Abbreviation for Colonel

COP- Combat Outpost

Cordon- A area that has been blocked or secured

Corpsman- Navy Medic

Dari- Afghan tribal language

DEMO- Demolitions or Explosives

DET- Detonation or Detonation Cord

Devil Dog- Slang term for Marine

DM- Designated Marksman

DNA- Acid molecule that carry's individual genetic material

DOD- Dept. of Defense

DUSHKA- A BFG, 12.7mm machine gun (bug fucking gun)

ECP- Entry control point

EOD- Explosive Ordinance Disposal

E tool- Small foldable shovel (they suck)

FAC- Forward Air Controller

FAG- British slang or term for cigarette

FLIR- Forward Looking Infrared, optic

FOB- Forward Operating Base

Fobbit- Slang term for being stuck on a FOB

FML- Fuck My Life!

GIROA- Government of the Islamic Republic of Afghanistan

God's Eye- A type or surveillance platform using a balloon

GOV Affairs- Government or Governmental Affairs

GP- General Purpose

Green Mile- Area of Helmond wadi where INDIA killed and blew shit up

Hashish- Processed type of Marijuana

Hellfire- Air to Surface missile for precision strikes

HELO- Helicopter

HESCO- Protective barrier, cloth material wrapped with thick wire, filled with dirt

HIMARS- High Mobility Artillery Rocket System rocket launcher

Hotwash- A quick down and dirty SITREP

HME- Homemade Explosive

HUMINT- Human or person based Intelligence source

IDF Indirect Fire

IDF- Indirect Fire

IFAK- Individual First Aid Kit

J- Slang term for jungle

JUMP- Marine Close Protection Unit

Javelin- U.S. Military anti-tank missile

Jungle- the term used to describe the vast crop fields

K9- A military or police working dog

KAF- Kandahar Air Field, Afghanistan

KLE- Key leader engagement

Klick- Unit of measure for distance, one kilometer

LAW- Light anti-armor weapon

LCPL- Abbreviation for Lance Corporal

LCPL Pipeline- The place where all rumors start and end in the Marine Corps

LEP- Law Enforcement Professional

LOGCAP- Logistic Capability or Civil Augmentation Program

LT- Lieutenant

LTC- Lieutenant Colonel

LZ- Landing Zone

M4- Shortened version of M16 Rifle, select fire

M16- U.S. Military combat rifle, select fire

M203- 40mm Grenade launcher

M240/240- U.S. Military 7.62 machine gun

M249- SAW 5.56 machine gun

Ma Deuce- Slang term for 50 caliber, machine gun (Thank you John Moses Browning)

Mag- A weapon magazine that holds and feeds rounds of ammunition

Man Ass- Slang term for Manas, Kyrgyzstan Air Field

Marijuana- That weed you smoke to get high

Meth- Slang for Methamphetamine

Meth Monkey- Police slang for an addict of Methamphetamine

MGUNS- Master Gunnery Sergeant

MICLIC- Mine Clearing Line Charge, explosive vehicle/trailer mounted

MK19- U.S. Military Automatic Grenade launcher, (they rock)

Mojave Viper- Marine Infantry Readiness Exercise, desert style

Mosque- Muslim Holy Place for prayer

MRAP- Mine Resistant Ambush Protected vehicle

MRE- pre-packaged Meals Ready to Eat, yummy!

Muzzle thump- Slang for thumping bad guys with the front muzzle of a weapon

Navy Cross- 2nd Highest U.S. Military Award for Valor given under the Naval Service

NCIS- Naval Criminal Investigative Service

NCO- Enlisted non-commissioned officer

NDS- Afghanistan's National Directorate of Security

NOD- Night Optic Device

No Go- Slang for not good or not doable

Nut Sack Mag- A cloth or canvas type machine gun magazine

NVG's- Night Vision Googles

Old Chesty- Chesty Puller, Famous Marine War Legend, 5x Navy Crosses

OOHRAH- Marine term used for motivation or ass whooping

OMG- Oh My God!

Ops- Operations

OP's O- Operations Officer

Overwatch- A security position from a vantage point from above the person/place

Pashto- Afghan tribal language

Pavehawk- Military type helicopter

PB- Patrol Base

PSYOPS- Psychological Operations

PGOV- Provincial Governor

PB- Patrol Base

PETN- Peroxide based explosive

PFC- Private First Class

PID- Positive Identification

PKM- Russian Bloc machine gun, 7.62x54mm

PMAG- A polymer magazine

POG- Person other than Grunt

POO- Point of Origin, not poop

POI- Point of Impact

PPE- Personal Protective Equipment

PSD- Personal Security Detail

P/U- Pick up

PT- Physical training

PTSD- Post Traumatic Stress Disorder

Qualat/Qalat- Type of mud structure or compound found in the Middle East region

Q & A- Questions and Answers

QRF- Quick Reaction Force

RAH- Shorter version of OOHRAH

Ratfucked- Marine term or slang for an item that has been gone through

Redneck- Me the LEP

ROE- Rule of Engagement

RPG- Rocket propelled grenade

RPK- Russian Bloc machine gun, 7.62x39mm

Rubber Bitch- A rolled up sleeping pad, solid or inflatable

SA- Situational Awareness

SAF- Small arms fire

SAS- British Special Forces, Special Air Service

SAT phone- Satellite telephone

SAW- M249 Squad Automatic Weapon 5.56

SBS- British Special Forces, Special Boat Service

SF- Special Forces

SGT- Abbreviation for Sergeant

SGTMAJ- Sergeant Major

Shadow- 3/7 Call Sign for sniper element

SITREP- Situation Report

Silver Star- 3rd Highest U.S. Military Award for Valor

SMAW- Shoulder launched multi-purpose assault weapon

SME- Subject Matter Expert

SNCO- Enlisted Staff level non-commissioned officer

SOCOM- Special Operations Command

SSGT- Abbreviation for Staff Sergeant

Stumps- Marine slang for 29 Palms, California

Taliban- Insurgent fighters from Afghanistan

TB- Slang for Taliban

TBI- Traumatic Brain Injury

TERP- Abbreviation for Interpreter

TIC- Troops in Contact

TOC- Tactical Operations Center

TOW- Anti-tank missile system

TQ- Tactical Questioning

Trash- Personal items of gear, equipment or things

Trow- Trousers

TSE- Tactical Site Exploitation

TTP- Tactics, Techniques and Procedures

VIC- Vehicle or Vehicle Commander

Willy Pete- A White Phosphorus grenade, high heat

WPNS- Weapons or Weapons Company

WTF- What the Fuck?

X- A bad place to be, where the bombs or bullets fly

XO- Executive Officer

ZZZZ's- Sleep

Made in the USA
San Bernardino, CA
01 May 2018